THE BEAUTIFUL GAME

JOHN ANDREWS has been a writer and editor since the days when Everton actually won things. He has contributed to many food and travel guides, including the *Good Food Guide*, written on sport, music, history and popular culture for Reader's Digest and Dorling Kindersley, and set countless quiz questions on all things sporty.

DANIEL NYARI is a Romanian-born illustrator living in New York City. He is creative director at FutbolArtistNetwork and is the co-founder and designer at Supporters.Pro. His work has been featured in the *New York Times, FourFourTwo, Wired, Süddeutsche Zeitung,* the *Guardian* and many other global publications.

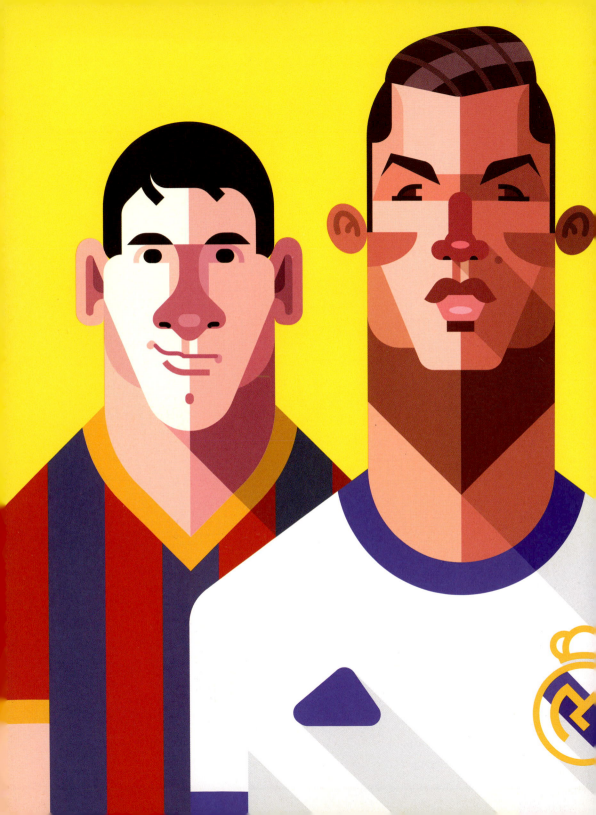

THE BEAUTIFUL GAME

JOHN ANDREWS

WITH PLAYER PORTRAITS BY

DANIEL NYARI

Aurum
Press

CONTENTS

IT ALL BEGAN IN SHEFFIELD

You could say that football, as we know it, started in the 1840s at the University of Cambridge, where the first rules – the Cambridge Rules – were drawn up. But club football really began in the Yorkshire city of Sheffield in 1857, spreading rapidly through the industrial heartlands of Britain and then around the world.

WORLD'S FIRST XI OLDEST CLUBS*

Not associated with schools, universities or armed forces, and continuously active. All in England, except for Wrexham (Wales) and Queen's Park (Scotland).

1857	**Sheffield FC**
1860	**Hallam FC**
1860	**Cray Wanderers FC**
1861	**Worksop Town FC**
1862	**Notts County FC ****
1863	**Stoke City FC**
1864	**Brigg Town FC**
1864	**Wrexham FC**
1865	**Nottingham Forest FC**
1867	**Queen's Park FC**
1867	**Sheffield Wednesday FC**

* some foundation dates are open to dispute
** world's oldest professional league club

OLDEST CLUB IN THE NETHERLANDS

1879 Koninklijke HFC (Haarlem)
The oldest Dutch professional club is Sparta Rotterdam, founded in 1888.

OLDEST CLUB IN ITALY

1893 Genoa CFC
Originally Genoa Cricket and Athletic Club, founded by British expats.

OLDEST CLUB IN GERMANY

1888 BFC Germania 1888 (Berlin)
Don't be fooled by names such as TSV 1860 Munich and SSV Ulm 1846 – many German football teams were founded first as gymnastics or athletics clubs and then took up football at a later date.

OLDEST CLUB IN FRANCE

1872 Le Havre AC

OLDEST CLUB IN SPAIN

1889 Recreativo de Huelva
Sevilla FC, founded in 1890, is the oldest top-flight Spanish club.

OLDEST CLUB IN PORTUGAL

1887 **Associação Académica de Coimbra**

OLDEST CLUB IN SWITZERLAND

1879 **FC St Gallen**

OLDEST CLUBS IN ASIA

1886 **Hong Kong FC** (China, Hong Kong)
1889 **Mohun Bagan AC** (India, Kolkata)
1904 **South China AA** (China, Hong Kong)
1917 **Tokyo Soccer Club** (Japan)

OLDEST CLUBS IN NORTH AMERICA

1898 **Beadling Soccer Club** (USA, Pittsburgh)
1901 **CF Pachuca*** (Mexico)
1909 **United Weston FC** (Canada, Winnipeg)

* founded by miners, from Cornwall, England

OLDEST CLUBS IN SOUTH AMERICA

1875 **Club Mercedes** (Argentina)
1891 **Albion FC** (Uruguay, Montevideo)
1892 **Santiago Wanderers** (Chile)
1895 **Flamengo** (Brazil, Rio de Janeiro)
1902 **Club Olimpia** (Paraguay, Asunción)

Lima CFC (Peru) claims to have been founded in 1859, which would make it the second-oldest club in the world. No documents, though, exist from the time.

OLDEST CLUBS IN AFRICA

1907 **Al Ahly SC** (Egypt, Cairo)
1911 **FC Barreirense** (Cape Verde)
1911 **Zamalek SC** (Egypt, Giza)
1911 **Accra Hearts of Oak SC** (Ghana)
1914 **Al-Ittihad** (Egypt, Alexandria)
1919 **Espérance Sportive de Tunis** (Tunisia)

OLDEST CLUBS IN OCEANIA

1883 **Balgownie Rangers FC** (Australia)
1887 **North Shore United AFC** (New Zealand)

WHERE'S YOUR FLANNEL CAP, SON?

Oh, for the days of legalized pushing and handball! In 1858, the members of Sheffield FC – the world's oldest football club – wrote down a simple set of rules for the game of 'foot-ball', which was beginning to move beyond English public schools and into the industrial north. Some rules look familiar, others certainly don't …

LAWS

FOR THE GUIDANCE OF PLAYING MEMBERS

1. Kick off from middle must be a place kick.

2. Kick out must not be from more than 25 yards out of goal.

3. Fair Catch is a catch from any player, provided the Ball has not touched the ground, or has not been thrown direct from touch, and entitles to a free kick.

4. Charging is fair in case of a place kick (with the exception of a kick off) as soon as the player offers to kick, but he may always draw back, unless he has actually touched the Ball with his foot.

5. Pushing with the hands is allowed, but no hacking or tripping up is fair under any circumstances whatsoever.

6. No player may be held or pulled over.

7. It is not lawful to take the Ball off the ground (except in touch) for any purpose whatever.

8. The Ball may be pushed or hit with the hand, but holding the Ball (except in the case of a fair kick) is altogether disallowed.

9. A goal must be kicked, but not from touch, nor by a free kick from a catch.

10. A Ball in touch is dead, consequently the side that touches it down must bring it to the edge of touch, and throw it straight out at least six yards from touch.

11. That each player must provide himself with a red and a dark blue flannel cap.   One colour to be worn by each side during play.

IT'S A EUROPEAN KNOCKOUT

We've won the cup! Despite the prestige and sheer long-distance excellence of winning one of Europe's big leagues, there's nothing quite like the unpredictable excitement generated by a cup competition, where the mighty can fall and the unexpected find glory. Will this be the year your club lifts the trophy?

ENGLAND

FA CUP
Founded 1871:
The Football Association Challenge Cup
736 teams
Most wins Arsenal and Manchester United (12)

EFL CUP
Founded 1960: originally called the Football League Cup
Most wins Liverpool (8)

FRANCE

COUPE DE FRANCE
Founded 1917:
Coupe Charles Simon
8,506 teams
Most wins Olympique de Marseille and Paris Saint-Germain (10)

COUPE DE LA LIGUE
Founded 1994
42 teams (from 3 leagues)
Most wins Paris Saint-Germain (6)

GERMANY

**DFB-POKAL
(GERMAN FOOTBALL FEDERATION CUP)**
Founded 1935:
Tschammer-Pokal
64 teams
Most wins Bayern Munich (18)

UEFA CHAMPIONS LEAGUE
Founded 1955:
European Champion Clubs' Cup
32 teams (group stage)
Winner prize €15.5m
Most wins Real Madrid (11)
Winners by nation:
16 Spain
12 Italy
12 England
7 Germany
6 Netherlands
4 Portugal
1 France, Scotland, Romania, Yugoslavia

SPAIN

**COPA DEL REY
(KING'S CUP)**
Founded 1903
83 teams
Most wins Barcelona (28)

SUPERCOPA DE ESPAÑA
Founded 1982
2 teams (winner of La Liga and
winner or runner-up
of Copa del Rey)
Most wins Barcelona (12)

ITALY

COPPA ITALIA
Founded 1922: currently
known as TIM Cup
78 teams
Most wins Juventus (11)

SUPERCOPPA ITALIANA
Founded 1988
2 teams (winner of Serie A
and winner or runner-up of
Coppa Italia)
Most wins Juventus (7)

NETHERLANDS

**KNVB BEKER
(ROYAL NETHERLANDS
FOOTBALL ASSOCIATION
CUP)**
Founded 1898
103 teams
Most wins Ajax (18)

**JOHAN CRUIJFF SCHAAL
(JOHAN CRUYFF SHIELD)**
Founded 1949: Super Cup
2 teams (winner of the KNVB
Beker and winner or runner-up
of the Eredivisie)
Most wins PSV Eindhoven (11)

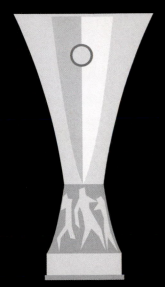

UEFA EUROPA LEAGUE
Founded 1971: UEFA Cup
48 teams (group stage, with
8 further teams after Champions
League group stage)
Winner prize €6.5m
Most wins Sevilla (5)
Winners by nation:
10 Spain
9 Italy
7 England
6 Germany
4 Netherlands
2 Russia, Portugal
1 Belgium, Turkey, Ukraine

TURKEY   **TURKISH CUP** (founded 1962)
Most wins Galatasaray (17)

UKRAINE   **UKRANIAN CUP** (founded 1992)
Most wins Dynamo Kiev (11)

RUSSIA   **RUSSIAN CUP** (founded 1992)
Most wins CSKA Moscow (7)

BELGIUM   **BELGIAN CUP** (founded 1911)
Most wins Club Brugge (11)

SWITZERLAND   **SWISS CUP** (founded 1926)
Most wins Grasshopper Club Zürich (19)

SCOTLAND   **SCOTTISH CUP** (founded 1873)
Most wins Celtic (36)

PORTUGAL   **PORTUGUESE CUP** (founded 1938)
Most wins Benfica (25)

THE WHOLE EUROPEAN CHAMPIONSHIP

Although first proposed in 1927, it was not until 1960 that a championship of European nations materialized, with 4 teams reaching the finals from a field of 17. Now, 24 countries battle it out in perhaps the most prestigious tournament after the World Cup. Here are all the entrants – some with names overtaken by history.

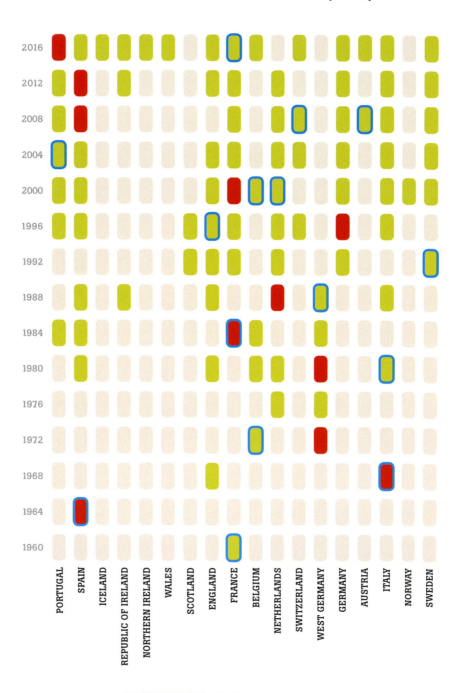

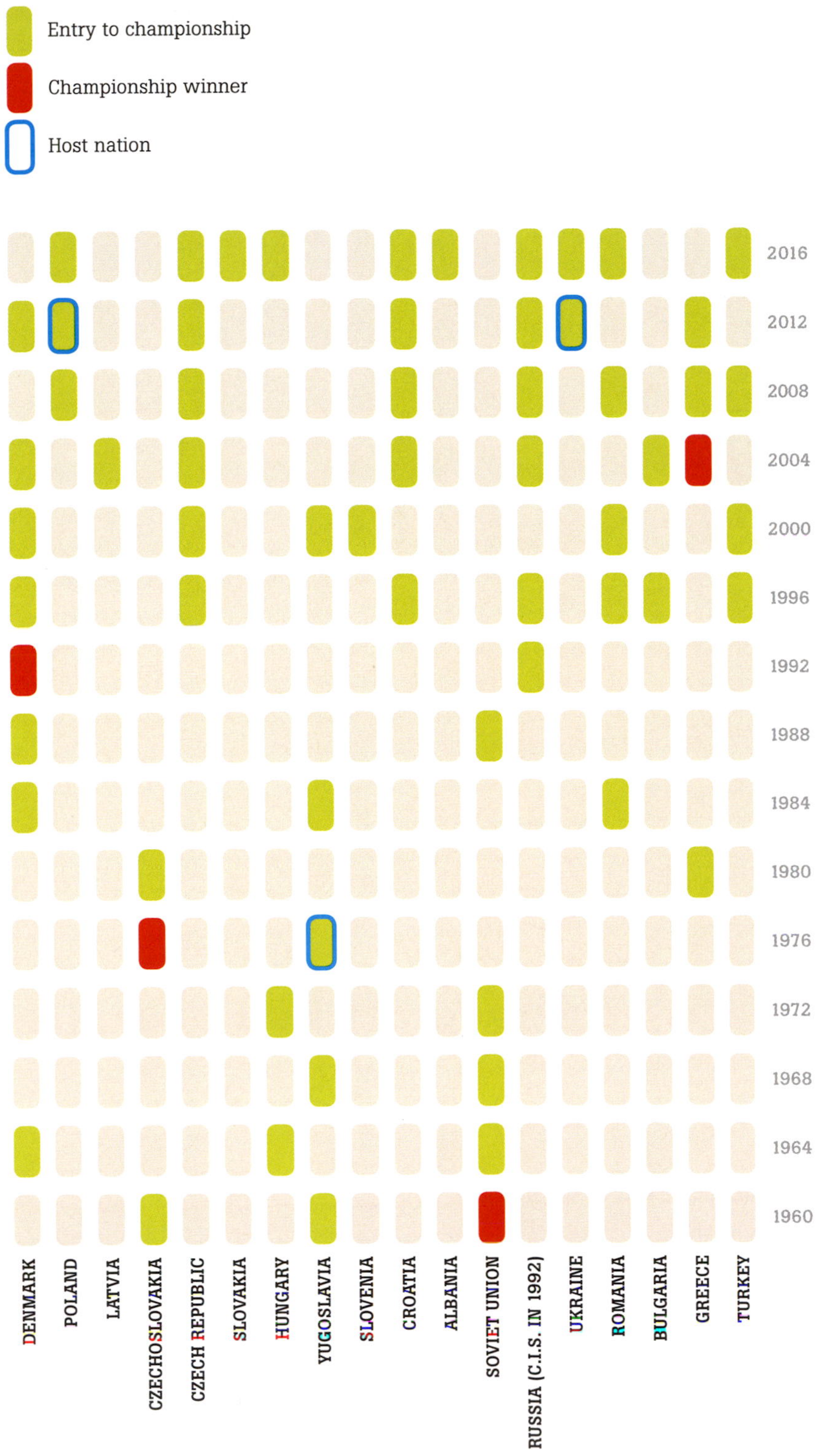

Entry to championship
Championship winner
Host nation

	DENMARK	POLAND	LATVIA	CZECHOSLOVAKIA	CZECH REPUBLIC	SLOVAKIA	HUNGARY	YUGOSLAVIA	SLOVENIA	CROATIA	ALBANIA	SOVIET UNION	RUSSIA (C.I.S. IN 1992)	UKRAINE	ROMANIA	BULGARIA	GREECE	TURKEY	
2016		■		■	■	■	■		■	■			■	■	■			■	2016
2012	■	▢		■			■					■		▢		■			2012
2008		■		■			■						■	■		■	■		2008
2004	■			■								■				■	■		2004
2000	■			■			■	■				■		■	■		■		2000
1996	■			■								■		■	■	■			1996
1992	■							■				■							1992
1988	■							■				■							1988
1984	■							■				■							1984
1980				■													■		1980
1976				■				▢											1976
1972							■					■							1972
1968							■					■							1968
1964	■						■												1964
1960				■			■					■							1960

15

DASHING DRIBBLERS

They're quick, dynamic, a defender's nightmare and the darlings of the fans. But who's the fastest of all dribblers? Well, according to a study carried out in 2015 by the Mexican top-tier club Pachuca and backed by FIFA, these are the top 10 of today's tearaways.

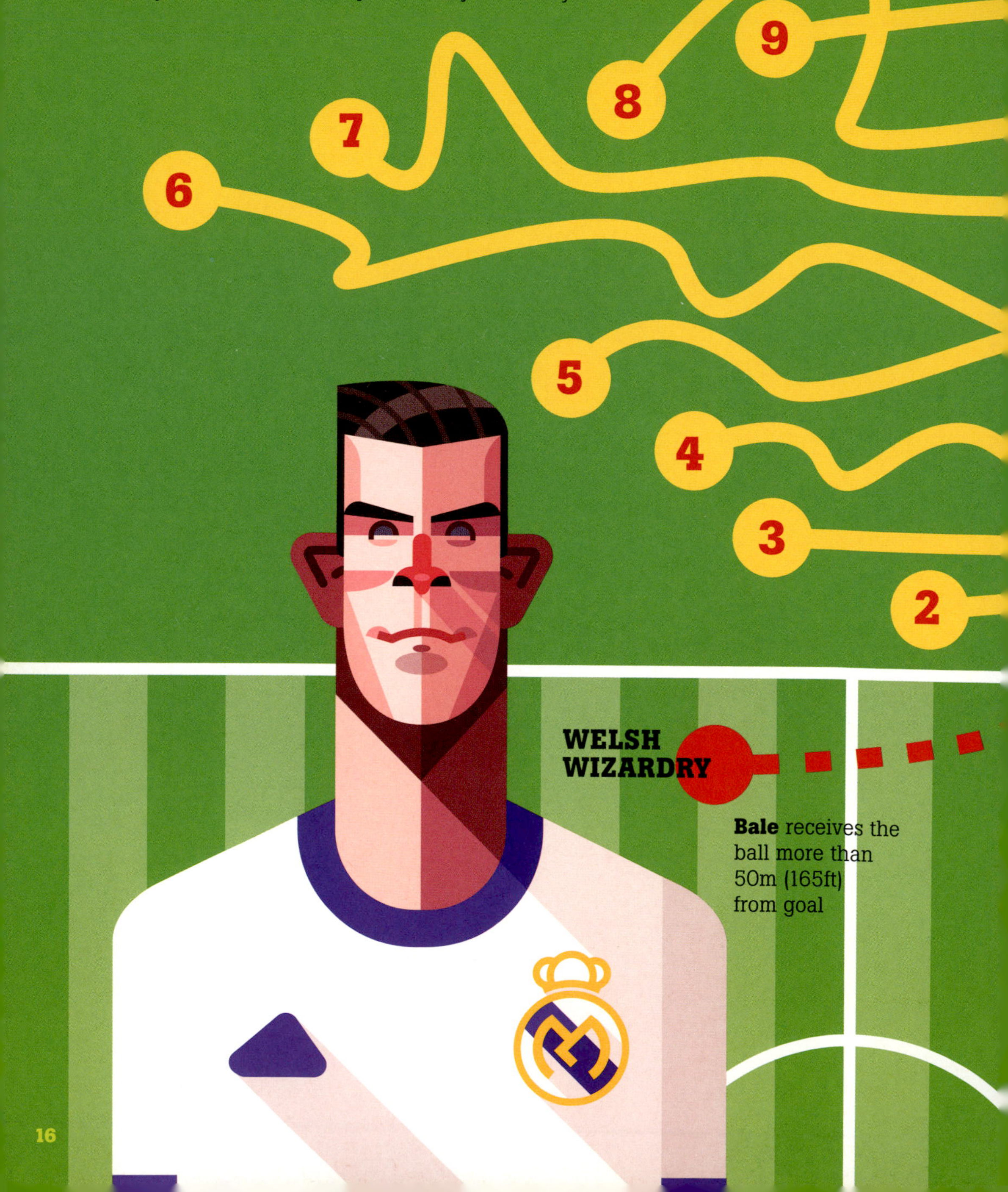

10

9

8

7

6

5

4

3

2

WELSH WIZARDRY

Bale receives the ball more than 50m (165ft) from goal

Sergio Ramos
Real Madrid
30.6 km/h (19 mph)

Franck Ribéry
Bayern Munich
30.7 km/h (19.1 mph)

Wayne Rooney
Manchester United
31.2 km/h (19.4 mph)

Lionel Messi
Barcelona
32.5 km/h (20.2 mph)

Cristiano Ronaldo
Real Madrid
33.6 km/h (20.9 mph)

Theo Walcott
Arsenal
32.7 km/h (20.3 mph)

Aaron Lennon
Everton
33.8 km/h (21 mph)

Antonio Valencia
Manchester United
35.1 km/h (21.8 mph)

Jürgen Damm
Tigres UANL
35.23 km/h (21.9 mph)

Bartra pushes
Bale off the pitch

Bale races beyond
Bartra on the outside

1 **GARETH BALE**
Real Madrid
36.9 km/h (22.9 mph)
Gareth Bale's stunning individual goal
5 minutes from time won the 2014 Copa del
Rey for Real Madrid as they beat archrivals
Barcelona 2–1 in Valencia. The Wales
forward outsprinted Barca defender Marc
Bartra from the halfway line before coolly
converting past keeper José Manuel Pinto.

7.2 seconds
later Bale
shoots past
Pinto to score

GOAL!

KEEPERS ARE DIFFERENT

They're a crazy bunch, but top goalkeepers win matches just as much as staunch defenders, midfield maestros or prolific strikers. It's the loneliest, most exposed position on the pitch, so put your big, gloved hands together and show your appreciation for some great shot-stoppers.

Dino Zoff

1,142 Minutes between goals conceded in international matches 1972–74 – a world record
6 Serie A titles with Juventus
4 World Cups
40 Years of age when captain of Italy in 1982 – the oldest World Cup final player

Goal!

Pele's cry as he heads the ball at England's net in the 1970 World Cup, only for Gordon Banks to make football's most famous save.

Gordon Banks

442 Minutes before Banks conceded a goal at the 1966 World Cup finals
7 Clean sheets up to the 1966 semifinal
1 Bottle of suspect beer that kept Banks out of the 1970 World Cup quarterfinal against West Germany, which England lost 3-2

Sepp Maier

95 Caps for West Germany – more than any other German keeper
422 Consecutive games for Bayern Munich – a Bundesliga record
4 Goals conceded on the way to West Germany's 1974 World Cup victory

Peter Schmeichel

22 Clean sheets during Manchester United's 1992–93 Premier League-winning season
42 Per cent of Premier League games with clean sheets
129 Caps for Denmark, a national record
1st Keeper to score in the Premier League – for Aston Villa against Everton in 2001

Lev Yashin

150+ Spot kicks saved
270 Clean sheets
1963 Year Yashin became the only keeper to win the Ballon d'Or for European footballer of the year
12 Years it took Russia to qualify for the World Cup following Yashin's retirement
326 Games for Dynamo Moscow between 1950 and 1970

'Black Spider'
The nickname given to Yashin for his all-black strip and his ability to seemingly save everything.

GOALIE GOBSMACKERS

31 Goals let in by Nicky Salapu of American Samoa against Australia in a 2001 World Cup-qualifying game

0 Goals conceded by Swiss keeper Pascal Zuberbühler over 463 minutes of football in the 2006 World Cup – the only clean sheet kept throughout a tournament

3 Keepers who have captained their sides to World Cup victory: Giampiero Combi (Italy 1934), Dino Zoff (Italy 1982) and Iker Casillas (Spain 2010)

181 Caps won by Mohamed Al-Deayea for Saudi Arabia – the international record

16 Saves made by Tim Howard of USA against Belgium in the 2014 World Cup – no one has topped that

921 Minutes New Zealand keeper Richard Wilson went without conceding a goal in his country's 1982 World Cup qualifying campaign

Manuel Neuer

Goalie great in the making The leader of a new generation of 'sweeper-keepers', Neuer (born 1986) already has a Golden Glove award and winner's medal for the 2014 World Cup, and a third place in the 2014 Ballon d'Or – a rarity for a keeper. He is rated by many as the best since Lev Yashin.

FOLLICALLY CHALLENGED!

Hair today, gone tomorrow – while some footballers like to tease their locks into statement styles, others have no choice but to let nature have its way and take to the field as bald as the day they were born. Some of football's greats have had smooth, shiny pates – certainly more than enough to make up an impressive follicle-free fantasy XI.

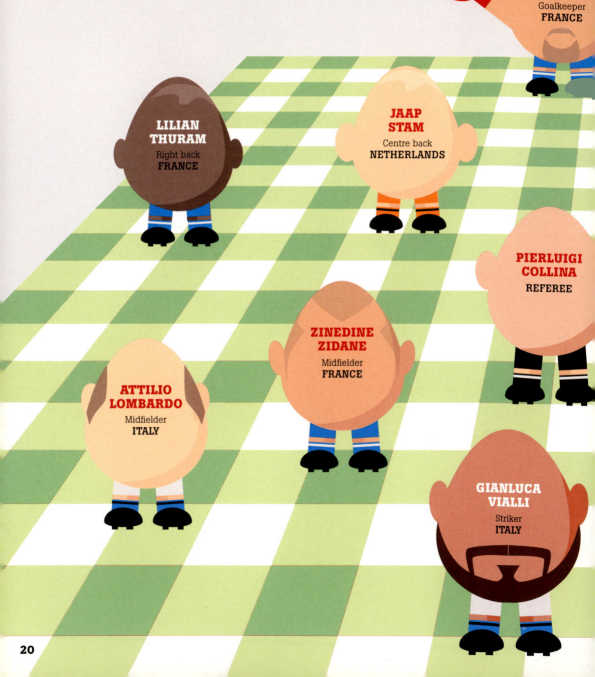

FABIEN BARTHEZ
Goalkeeper
FRANCE

LILIAN THURAM
Right back
FRANCE

JAAP STAM
Centre back
NETHERLANDS

PIERLUIGI COLLINA
REFEREE

ZINEDINE ZIDANE
Midfielder
FRANCE

ATTILIO LOMBARDO
Midfielder
ITALY

GIANLUCA VIALLI
Striker
ITALY

SUBS
Brad Friedel (USA)
Wayne Rooney (pre-transplant – England)
Jan Koller (Czech Republic)
Temur Ketsbaia (Georgia)
Esteban Cambiasso (Argentina)
Clarence Seedorf (Netherlands)
Fabio Cannavaro (Italy)
Thierry Henry (France)
Freddie Ljungberg (Sweden)
Carsten Jancker (Germany)

MANAGER
Pep Guardiola (Spain)

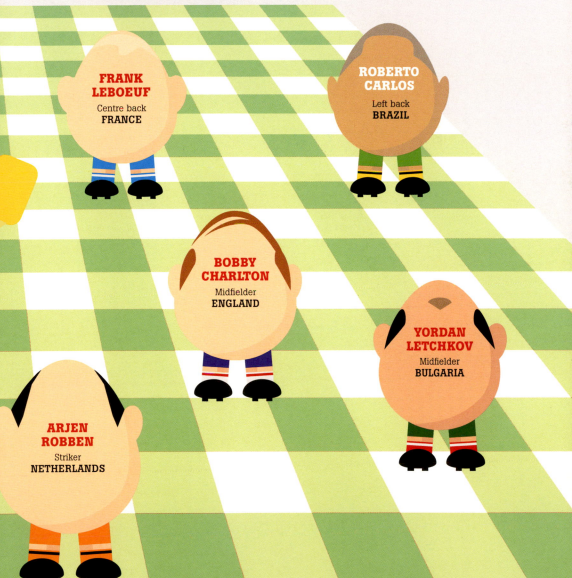

FRANK LEBOEUF
Centre back
FRANCE

ROBERTO CARLOS
Left back
BRAZIL

BOBBY CHARLTON
Midfielder
ENGLAND

YORDAN LETCHKOV
Midfielder
BULGARIA

ARJEN ROBBEN
Striker
NETHERLANDS

WHO RULES THE WORLDS?

'An African nation will win the World Cup before the year 2000,' said Pelé – last century. How wrong he was. The World Cup has been dominated by countries from just two continents – Europe and South America – with the rest hardly figuring, from winner right down to fourth place. And it's one from each of those two continents, Germany and Brazil, that top the achievement pile.

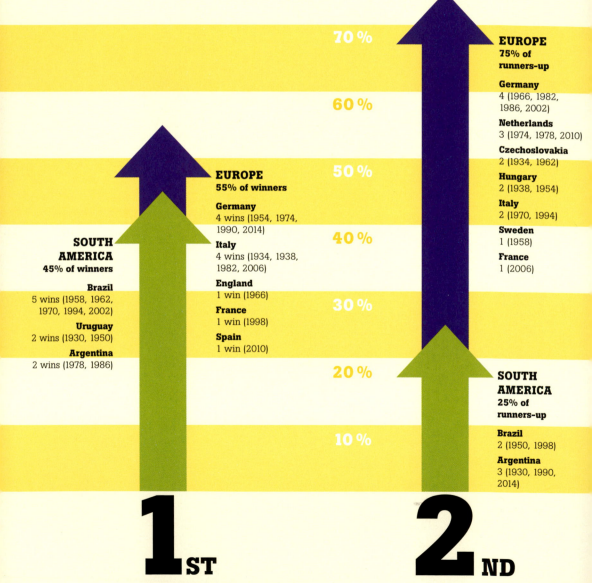

EUROPE

SOUTH AMERICA

REST OF WORLD

80 %

70 %

60 %

50 %

40 %

30 %

20 %

10 %

EUROPE
75% of runners-up

Germany
4 (1966, 1982, 1986, 2002)

Netherlands
3 (1974, 1978, 2010)

Czechoslovakia
2 (1934, 1962)

Hungary
2 (1938, 1954)

Italy
2 (1970, 1994)

Sweden
1 (1958)

France
1 (2006)

EUROPE
55% of winners

Germany
4 wins (1954, 1974, 1990, 2014)

Italy
4 wins (1934, 1938, 1982, 2006)

England
1 win (1966)

France
1 win (1998)

Spain
1 win (2010)

SOUTH AMERICA
45% of winners

Brazil
5 wins (1958, 1962, 1970, 1994, 2002)

Uruguay
2 wins (1930, 1950)

Argentina
2 wins (1978, 1986)

SOUTH AMERICA
25% of runners-up

Brazil
2 (1950, 1998)

Argentina
3 (1930, 1990, 2014)

1ST

2ND

TOP FOUR FINISHERS

13 GERMANY
11 BRAZIL
8 ITALY
5 ARGENTINA
5 NETHERLANDS
5 URUGUAY

80 %

70 %

EUROPE
80% of 3rd
placed teams

Germany
4 (1934, 1970, 2006, 2010)

60 %

Sweden
2 (1950, 1994)

France
2 (1958, 1986)

Poland
2 (1974, 1982)

50 %

Austria
1 (1954)

Portugal
1 (1966)

Italy
1 (1990)

40 %

Croatia
1 (1998)

Turkey
1 (2002)

30 %

Netherlands
1 (2014)

EUROPE
70% of 4th
placed teams

Yugoslavia
2 (1930, 1962)

Austria
1 (1934)

Sweden
1 (1938)

Spain
1 (1950)

Germany
1 (1958)

Soviet Union
1 (1966)

Italy
1 (1978)

France
1 (1982)

Belgium
1 (1986)

England
1 (1990)

20 %

SOUTH
AMERICA
25% of 4th
placed teams

Bulgaria
1 (1994)

Netherlands
1 (1998)

Uruguay
3 (1954, 1970, 2010)

Portugal
1 (2006)

10 %

SOUTH
AMERICA
15% of 3rd
placed teams

Brazil
2 (1974, 2014)

REST OF WORLD
5% of 3rd
placed teams

Brazil
2 (1938, 1978)

Chile
1 (1962)

USA
1 (1930)

REST OF WORLD
5% of 4th
placed teams

South Korea
1 (2002)

3RD

4TH

23

ZERO TOLERANCE

Why do they put themselves through it – those mostly tiny nations that have barely enough people to fill a stadium, let alone field a football team capable of stopping the tsunami of goals heading their way? Well, play those plucky players do, providing bigger teams with easy meat. For the silliest score, though, you need to look at some Madagascan league skulduggery …

46–0

VANUATU 46–0 MICRONESIA

2015, Pacific Games

- 16 – goals scored by Jean Kaltack, the most by one player in an international game
- 38–0 – the defeat Micronesia suffered at the hands of Fiji only two days earlier … oh, and there was the small matter of a 30–0 defeat to Tahiti two days before that. Quite a week …

0–13

SAN MARINO 0–13 GERMANY

2006, European Championship qualifier

- Record defeat for any team in the European Championship
- San Marino ended the 12-game qualifying round with a goal difference of -55
- Lukas Podolski notched up 4 goals
- San Marino's population of 31,000 is more than 2,500 times smaller than that of Germany, though the 5,000 match crowd represented an impressively high proportion of the microstate's people

BIGGEST WORLD CUP ZEROS

Sweden 8–0 Cuba (1938) >> Hungary 9–0 South Korea (1954) >>

30–0

TAHITI 30–0 COOK ISLANDS
1971, South Pacific Games
- Cook Islands did a little better in their next game, losing only 16–1 to Papua New Guinea
- Cook Islands' population is 15,000 (2011 census)

149–0

AS ADEMA 149–0 STADE OLYMPIQUE DE L'EMYRNE
2002, Madagascar league
- All goals were own goals
- Stade Olympique De L'Emyrne players were protesting at a refereeing decision they thought had gone against them in the national championship play-offs
- This is the world record professional football scoreline

31–0

AUSTRALIA 31–0 AMERICAN SAMOA
2001, World Cup Oceania qualifier
- 13 – goals scored by Archie Thompson
- 15 – the age of two of the American Samoa players
- 1 – shots on target from American Samoa

ugoslavia 9–0 Zaire (1974)   >>   Germany 8–0 Saudi Arabia (2002)

OLD ENOUGH TO SHAVE YET?

Most footballers don't reach their peak until well into their 20s. Some precocious types, though, are thrust onto the world stage when their friends are still at school. A select few, like a certain 17-year-old Edson Arantes do Nascimento (aka Pelé), go on to greatness, while others never quite fulfill that early potential.

THE YOUNG ONES

23 years – age of **Bodo Illgner**, the youngest goalkeeper to appear in a World Cup-winning team, Germany, in 1990; he was also the first goalkeeper to keep a clean sheet in a World Cup final, helping Germany to a 1-0 victory over Argentina

14 years, 154 days – age of **Kreshnik Krasniqi** when he made his debut for Honefass on 25 May 2015 in the Norwegian first division

15 years, 300 days – age of **Martin Ødegaard**, who became the youngest player in the history of the European Championship when he came on as a subsititute for Norway in a 2-1 victory over Bulgaria in October 2014

12 years, 362 days – age of **Mauricio Baldivieso**, when, on 19 July 2009, he came on as a substitute for Bolivian league side Aurora and became the youngest person ever to play professional football

25.7 years – average age of the Argentinian team that won the 1978 World Cup: the youngest ever

the only way is up ...

PELÉ

17 years, 239 days

Pelé's age when he scored for Brazil in the quarterfinal of the 1958 World Cup: the youngest ever World Cup scorer

20 YOUNGEST TO HAVE PLAYED IN A WORLD CUP MATCH

		COUNTRY	DATE	POSITION	AGE Years-Months-Days
1	NORMAN WHITESIDE	Northern Ireland	17/06/1982	*Midfielder/striker*	17-01-10
2	SAMUEL ETO'O	Cameroon	17/06/1998	*Striker*	17-03-07
3	FEMI OPABUNMI	Nigeria	12/06/2002	*Midfielder*	17-03-09
4	SALOMON OLEMBÉ	Cameroon	11/06/1998	*Midfielder*	17-06-03
5	PELÉ	Brazil	15/06/1958	*Midfielder/striker*	17-07-23
6	BARTHOLOMEW OGBECHE	Nigeria	02/06/2002	*Striker*	17-08-01
7	RIGOBERT SONG	Cameroon	19/06/1994	*Defender*	17-11-18
8	CARVALHO LEITE	Brazil	20/07/1930	*Striker*	18-00-25
9	MANUEL ROSAS	Mexico	13/07/1930	*Midfielder*	18-02-26
10	CHRISTIAN ERIKSEN	Denmark	14/06/2010	*Midfielder*	18-04-00
11	BERTUS DE HARDER	Netherlands	05/06/1938	*Striker*	18-04-22
12	VINCENT ABOUBAKAR	Cameroon	19/06/2010	*Striker*	18-04-28
13	ASSIMIOU TOURÉ	Togo	13/06/2006	*Defender*	18-05-12
14	MICHAEL OWEN	England	15/06/1998	*Striker*	18-06-01
15	CHRIS WOOD	New Zealand	15/06/2010	*Striker*	18-06-08
16	GIUSEPPE BERGOMI	Italy	05/07/1982	*Defender*	18-06-13
17	NICOLAE KOVÁCS	Romania	14/07/1930	*Striker*	18-06-15
18	ANDRZEJ IWAN	Poland	06/06/1978	*Striker*	18-06-27
19	CARLOS IBÁÑEZ	Chile	02/07/1950	*Striker*	18-07-02
20	DMITRI SYCHEV	Russia	05/06/2002	*Striker*	18-07-10

EARLY LEARNERS

Baby Boomers – Cameroon has produced 4 out of the 20 youngest World Cup players (that's 20 per cent)

Young Guns – 13 of the 20 youngest Word Cup players have been strikers or attacking midfielders (that's 65 per cent)

0 – the number of goalkeepers in the youngest top 20

AGE CANNOT WITHER THEM

And, to further adapt the Shakespeare: 'nor custom stale their infinite variety'. Well, that certainly goes for the great players pushing, or on the wrong side of, 40, who have graced World Cups and beyond, making up for what they lack in youthful energy with the wiliness that comes only with age. Most, of course, are the sporadically active goalies, though some have still been scoring and creating goals when they should have been on TV-pundit duty or running a pub.

20 OLDEST TO HAVE PLAYED IN A WORLD CUP MATCH

		COUNTRY	DATE Last Played	POSITION	AGE Years-Months-Days
1	FARYD MONDRAGON	Colombia	24/06/2014	Goalkeeper	43-00-03
2	ROGER MILLA	Cameroon	28/06/1994	Striker	42-01-08
3	PAT JENNINGS	Northern Ireland	12/06/1986	Goalkeeper	41-00-00
4	PETER SHILTON	England	07/07/1990	Goalkeeper	40-09-19
5	DINO ZOFF	Italy	11/07/1982	Goalkeeper	40-04-13
6	ALI BOUMNIJEL	Tunisia	23/06/2006	Goalkeeper	40-02-10
7	JIM LEIGHTON	Scotland	23/06/1998	Goalkeeper	39-10-30
8	DAVID JAMES	England	27/06/2010	Goalkeeper	39-10-26
9	ÁNGEL LABRUNA	Argentina	15/06/1958	Striker	39-08-18
10	JOSEPH ANTOINE BELL	Cameroon	24/06/1994	Goalkeeper	39-08-16
11	STANLEY MATTHEWS	England	26/06/1954	Striker	39-04-25
12	JAN HEINTZE	Denmark	06/06/2002	Defender	38-09-20
13	DAVID SEAMAN	England	21/06/2002	Goalkeeper	38-09-02
14	VÍTOR DAMAS	Portugal	11/06/1986	Goalkeeper	38-08-03
15	MARIO YEPES	Colombia	04/07/2014	Defender	38-05-21
16	FERNANDO CLAVIJO	USA	04/07/1994	Defender	38-05-11
17	PAULO BENTO	Portugal	03/06/1986	Midfielder	37-11-09
18	RUSSELL LATAPY	Trinidad & Tobago	20/06/2006	Midfielder	37-10-18
19	MARK SCHWARZER	Australia	23/06/2010	Goalkeeper	37-08-17
20	GUNNAR GREN	Sweden	29/06/1958	Striker	37-07-29

YOU SHOULD TAKE IT EASY ...
8 out of the 10 oldest to play in World Cups have been goalkeepers
4 Strikers in the oldest top 20
0 Midfielders in the top 10, with only 2 in the top 20

OLDIES BUT GOLDIES

71 years The age of **Salvador Reyes**, a former Mexico striker, when he ran onto the field for Mexican club CD Guadalajara (Las Chivas) in 2008 – 41 years after he had last played. Reyes took the kick-off and was then substituted

Oldest professional footballer – **Kazuyoshi Miura** (1967–), who is a striker for Yokohama FC in the J2 League of the Japanese J.League. In 1994–95 he played for Genoa, the first Japanese footballer to appear in Serie A

55 years The age of goalkeeper **Dave Beasant** when he appeared as a sub on the bench for Stevenage Borough in a match against Carlisle United in October 2014 in the English League Two. At Wembley Stadium in 1988 Beasant became the first goalkeeper to save a penalty in an FA Cup Final, when Wimbledon defeated Liverpool 1–0

46 years, **7 months** and **4 days** The age of the oldest player in a World Cup qualifier: **MacDonald Taylor, Sr**, who turned out for US Virgin Islands against St Kitts and Nevis on 31 March 2004, only to lose 7–0

Oldest debutante in a World Cup tournament – **David James** (39 years, 10 months and 17 days) for England against Algeria, 18 June 2010

the only way is down ...

DINO ZOFF

Oldest player in a World Cup final
(40 years, 4 months and 13 days) for Italy against West Germany, 11 July 1982

FOOTBALL SCOUNDRELS

Love 'em or loathe 'em, the naughty nations and sinning stars who push the laws of the game to the limit – and beyond – spice up the world of football. Keep calm, and don't let this lot provoke you.

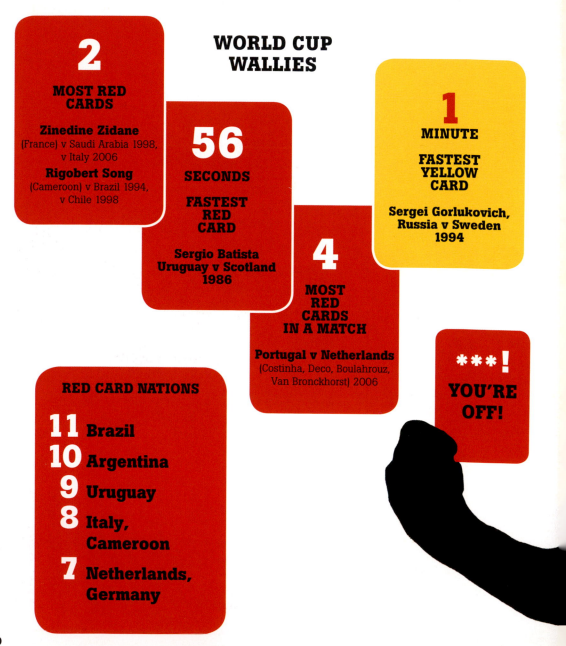

WORLD CUP WALLIES

2
MOST RED CARDS

Zinedine Zidane
(France) v Saudi Arabia 1998, v Italy 2006
Rigobert Song
(Cameroon) v Brazil 1994, v Chile 1998

56 SECONDS
FASTEST RED CARD

Sergio Batista
Uruguay v Scotland 1986

1 MINUTE
FASTEST YELLOW CARD

Sergei Gorlukovich, Russia v Sweden 1994

4
MOST RED CARDS IN A MATCH

Portugal v Netherlands
(Costinha, Deco, Boulahrouz, Van Bronckhorst) 2006

***!
YOU'RE OFF!

RED CARD NATIONS

11 Brazil
10 Argentina
9 Uruguay
8 Italy, Cameroon
7 Netherlands, Germany

7 DEADLY SINNERS

LUIS SUÁREZ (Uruguay) *Compulsive biter*
- Bite 1 – 2010, on Bakkal of PSV Eindhoven
- Bite 2 – 2013, on Ivanovic of Chelsea
- Bite 3 – 2014, on Chiellini of Italy

NEYMAR (Brazil) *Not so golden boy*
57 cards – 53 yellows, 4 reds (3 straight reds) in four years at Santos (2009–13)

PAUL SCHOLES (England) *British bulldog*
32 yellow cards in the Champions League – more than any other player
1 – only English player to be sent off (5 June 1999) at the old Wembley (1923–2003)

SERGIO RAMOS (Spain) *Seeing red*
19 – red cards total reached in March 2014, a record for Spain's La Liga (plus the small matter of 180 yellow cards)

EL-HADJI DIOUF (Senegal) *Spitting image*
3 – charges or fines that have been meted out to Diouf for spitting, including once at an 11-year-old Middlesbrough fan

DJIBRIL CISSÉ (France) *Scores or walks*
6 goals, 2 red cards in 8 games for QPR in the 2011–12 Premier League season – that's a goal or a dismissal for each game

KEVIN MUSCAT (Australia) *Hospital tackler*
123 yellow cards, 12 red – the tally of a 20-year playing career in England and Australia
£250,000 – the fine for his devilish tackle on Matty Holmes of Charlton Athletic in 1998

THEATRES OF NATIONAL DREAMS

The hopes of nations, and clubs, swirl around the pitch, tiers and terraces of this pick of architectural wonders, built or adapted to showcase and celebrate the beautiful game, and spread across four continents. These sporting nerve centres are steeped in an atmosphere and sense of football history that few other stadiums can match.

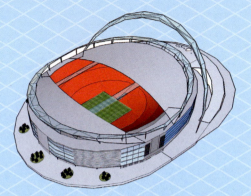

← WEMBLEY
LONDON, ENGLAND
Capacity **90,000** First game **2007**
The new Wembley stands on the site of the original stadium, which, along with its famous twin towers, was demolished in 2003. The 315m (1,033ft) span of the 133m (436ft) high arch makes it the longest single-span roof structure in the world. The seating rows, if placed end to end, would stretch 54km (33½ miles).

MARACANÃ →
RIO DE JANEIRO, BRAZIL
Capacity **78,639** First game **1950**
The Estádio Jornalista Mário Filho, known simply as the Maracanã, from its location in the Rio neighbourhood of the same name, was built to host the 1950 World Cup. A crowd of 174,000 (possibly many more) watched the final. Two clubs, Fluminense and Flamengo, also share the stadium.

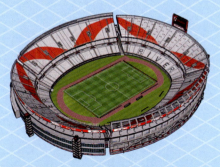

← ESTADIO MONUMENTAL
BUENOS AIRES, ARGENTINA
Capacity **61,688** First game **1938**
Named Estadio Antonio Vespucio Liberti after the River Plate club president who oversaw its construction, Argentina's main national stadium is more commonly known as El Monumental. It hosted the 1978 World Cup final, where Argentina beat the Netherlands 3–1.

ESTADIO AZTECA →
MEXICO CITY, MEXICO
Capacity **95,000** First game **1966**
Along with the Maracanã, the Azteca is the only stadium to have hosted two World Cup finals – in 1970 and 1986. It is also home to one of Mexico's most successful league teams, Club América, whose opponents have to cope with the Azteca's energy-sapping altitude of 2,240m (7,350ft).

OLYMPIASTADION →
BERLIN, GERMANY
Capacity **74,475** First game **1937**
The stadium was built as the centrepiece of the 1936 Berlin Olympics. It fell into gradual disrepair after the Second World War but was renovated in time for the 2006 World Cup, hosting the final between Italy and France. Bundesliga club Hertha BSC plays its home games at the stadium.

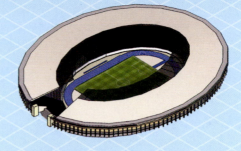

← FNB STADIUM
JOHANNESBURG, SOUTH AFRICA
Capacity **94,736** First game **1989**
Originally known as Soccer City, the stadium, Africa's largest, was redesigned for the 2010 World Cup and clad in a mosaic of earth and fire colours to resemble an African cooking pot. The stadium also serves as the home ground for the Kaizer Chiefs football club.

AZADI STADIUM →
TEHRAN, IRAN
Capacity **84,412** First game **1973**
The national Iranian stadium, the vast Azadi, with its sweeping structural curves, was built for the 1974 Asian Games. It also hosts one of the world's most heated and intense derbies, between Persepolis and Esteghlal – the two Tehran clubs that share the ground.

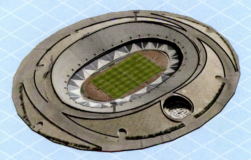

← LUZHNIKI STADIUM
MOSCOW, RUSSIA
Capacity **78,360** First game **1956**
The final of the 2018 World Cup will be held in the imposing Luzhniki, with capacity increased to 81,000 for the tournament. It is Russia's largest football stadium and was the focal point for the 1980 Moscow Olympics.

STADIO OLYMPICO →
ROME, ITALY
Capacity **70,634** First game **1953**
Scene of another passionate local derby, between Lazio and AS Roma, the two home clubs, the Stadio Olympico has hosted the 1960 Rome Olympics and the 1990 World Cup final between Germany and Argentina. The stadium is now also the venue for Italy's home rugby union fixtures.

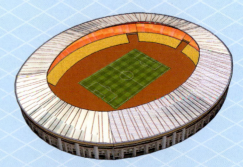

OUT OF AFRICA

An African nation may not have won the World Cup yet, but the Premier League, La Liga and other top club competitions are packed with great African players. Most of these get together every two years to compete in the Africa Cup of Nations, which has taken place 31 times since 1957.

[★ = final]

1957 SUDAN
★ Egypt 4 Ethiopia 0
- *3 teams only took part*
- *South Africa were disqualified from playing, giving Ethiopia a bye into the final – their only game*
- *4 goals scored in the final by Ad-Diba of Egypt*

1959 UNITED ARAB REPUBLIC (UAR)
★ UAR 2 Sudan 1
- *UAR was a confederation of Egypt and Syria*
- *Only 3 teams took part, in a round-robin competition*

1962 ETHIOPIA
★ Ethiopia 4 UAR 2
- *Ethiopia, qualifying as hosts, only had to beat Tunisia to get to the final*

1963 GHANA
★ Ghana 3 Sudan 0
- *6 teams took part, in 2 groups*

1965 TUNISIA
★ Ghana 3 Tunisia 2
- *First time since 1957 that the hosts had not won the cup*

1968 ETHIOPIA
★ Democratic Republic of Congo 1 Ghana 0
- *The winners had lost 2–1 to Ghana in an earlier round*

1970 SUDAN
★ Sudan 1 Ghana 0
- *Fourth consecutive final for Ghana*

1972 CAMEROON
★ Republic of Congo 3 Mali 2
- *First, and only, title for Republic of Congo*

1974 EGYPT
★ Zaire 2 Zambia 2
(replay: Zaire 2 Zambia 0)
- *The replay took place only two days after the final*
- *In 1971–97, Zaire was the name of Democratic Republic of Congo*

1976 ETHIOPIA
Winner: **Morocco**
Runner-up: **Guinea**
- *The winner was decided in a final round of 3 games involving the 4 top teams from the first stage of 2 groups*

1978 GHANA
★ Ghana 2 Uganda 0
- *Ivory Coast and Mali were disqualified during the qualification rounds – but no one knows why*

1980 NIGERIA
★ Nigeria 3 Algeria 0
- *Nigeria's first win*

1982 LIBYA
★ Ghana 1 Libya 1
(7–6 on penalties)
- *First penalty shoot-out final*

1984 IVORY COAST
★ Cameroon 3 Nigeria 1
- *Cameroon's first title, beating Algeria in a semifinal penalty shoot-out (5–4) on the way*

1986 EGYPT
★ Egypt 0 Cameroon 0
(5–4 on penalties)
- *Roger Milla of Cameroon was the tournament's top scorer with 4 goals*

1988 MOROCCO
★ Cameroon 1 Nigeria 0
- *A penalty from Emmanuel Kundé decided the outcome of the final*

1990 ALGERIA
★ Algeria 1 Nigeria 0
- *Repeat of the final from 1980, but with Algeria coming out on top this time*

1992 SENEGAL
★ Ivory Coast 0 Ghana 0
(11–10 on penalties)
- *The final's penalty shoot-out was the first in any major international tournament to feature every player who had been on the pitch at full time*

1994 TUNISIA
★ Nigeria 2 Zambia 1
• *In 1993, 18 Zambian players died in a plane crash whle travelling to a qualifying match against Senegal*

1996 SOUTH AFRICA
★ South Africa 2 Tunisia 0
• *This was the first time South Africa had played in the Africa Cup of Nations, having been banned since the inaugural tournament*

1998 BURKINA FASO
★ Egypt 2 South Africa 0
• *Egypt's fourth title*

2000 GHANA AND NIGERIA
★ Cameroon 2 Nigeria 2
(4–3 on penalties)
• *Shaun Bartlett of South Africa was the tournament's top scorer with 5 goals*

2004 TUNISIA
★ Tunisia 2 Morocco 1
• *First victory for Tunisia*

2006 EGYPT
★ Egypt 0 Ivory Coast 0
(4–2 on penalties)
• *The tournament's top scorer was Samuel Eto'o of Cameroon with 5 goals*

2008 GHANA
★ Egypt 1 Cameroon 0
• *Again, the tournament's top scorer was Samuel Eto'o of Cameroon with 5 goals*

2010 ANGOLA
★ Egypt 1 Ghana 0
• *Egypt recorded their seventh win, a record in the tournament, and did so winning every single game*

2012 GABON AND EQUATORIAL GUINEA
★ Zambia 0 Ivory Coast 0
(8–7 on penalties)
• *Zambia were surprise first-time winners*

2013 SOUTH AFRICA
★ Nigeria 1 Burkina Faso 0
• *The tournament was switched to an odd year to avoid clashing with the World Cup*

2015 EQUATORIAL GUINEA
★ Ivory Coast 0 Ghana 0
(9–8 on penalties)
• *The holders, Nigeria, were a surprise non-qualifier for the tournament*

2017 GABON
★ Cameroon 2 Egypt 1
• *Cameroon won their fourth title after a 15-year wait, moving ahead of Ghana but still behind Egypt*

WINNERS

7 Egypt
5 Cameroon
4 Ghana
3 Nigeria
2 Democratic Republic of Congo, Ivory Coast
1 Algeria, Republic of Congo, Ethiopia, Morocco, South Africa, Sudan, Tunisia, Zambia

★ 11 finals out of 31 have been won by the host nation
★ Of the past 19 finals, 8 were decided on penalties
★ Over those 19 finals, only 28 goals were scored, at an average of 1.47 goals per final

2002 MALI
★ Cameroon 0 Senegal 0
(3–2 on penalties)
• *Best player of the tournament was Rigobert Song of Cameroon*

ON ME 'EAD, SON!

There are players who rarely score with their head, while some – usually the taller ones – make a speciality of it. The skills and techniques involved are probably equal to a well-executed pass, shot or deft flick, and a flying header can be as much of a thing of beauty as a perfectly curled free kick. Give a nod to these classic World Cup examples of the art of the headed goal.

UWE SEELER

West Germany 3–2 England, Mexico 1970

A long punt into the box is met by Seeler, who, although facing away from goal, flexes his neck and sends the ball looping over Peter Bonetti into the England goal to level the score at 2–2 with only 8 minutes to go.

ZINEDINE ZIDANE

France 3–0 Brazil, France 1998

The World Cup final, hosts against favourites – the scene is set for someone to embrace glory. Step forward Zidane, who rocks Brazil with two sumptuous first-half headers from wickedly inswinging corners.

PÉLÉ

Brazil 4–1 Italy, Mexico 1970

Rivelino crosses from the left and the short-statured Pelé leaps like he has springs in his feet to head home at the far post to score the first goal against Italy in the final. This was also Brazil's 100th World Cup goal.

MARTIN DAHLIN

Sweden 3–1 Russia, USA 1994

Sweden reached the semifinals in the USA, losing 1–0 to Brazil, and went on to claim third place. Along the way, in a victory over Russia, Dahlin steamed into the box, threw himself at the ball and scored a spectacular flying header.

ROBIN VAN PERSIE

**Netherlands, Feyenoord, Arsenal,
Manchester United, Fenerbahçe**

Robin van Persie's stunning leaping header from the edge of the box to level the score against Spain was one of the highlights of the 2014 World Cup in Brazil.

YORDAN LETCHKOV

Bulgaria 2–1 Germany, USA 1994

Before Van Persie came along, this was the greatest World Cup diving header – a piledriver from Letchkov that won the quarterfinal. Bulgaria's first goal was a glorious free kick from Hristo Stoichkov.

CARLES PUYOL

Spain 1–0 Germany, South Africa 2010

It was going to take a special goal to break down the Germans' tight defence and take Spain into their first World Cup final. Step up Puyol, who roared into the German box to meet a corner and fire home a header of blistering power.

PAOLO ROSSI

Italy 3–2 Brazil, Spain 1982

Part of a hat-trick of goals in one of the most memorable World Cup games, Rossi's exquisite header, running on to a perfect cross from Antonio Cabrini, came after only 5 minutes. Rossi went on to score the first goal in the final.

JARED BORGETTI

Mexico 1–1 Italy, South Korea and Japan 2002

Borgetti scored 46 goals for Mexico, but this had to be his best. Closely marked and facing away from goal, he managed to leap, twist, defy most laws of physics and float a delicate header past Gianluigi Buffon.

THE LONG AND THE SHORT OF IT

Footballers come in all shapes and sizes. Being a beanpole can help if you're a goalie, while a short stature and low centre of gravity can be a bonus for running rings around a defender. It certainly did Maradonna – 1.65m (5ft 5in) high – no harm. From giant to pocket-sized, here are some of the world's tallest and shortest.

MARCIN GARUCH
1.54m (5ft ½in)
Poland: Midfielder
OFK Grbalj

DANIEL VILLALVA
1.55m (5ft 1in)
Argentina: Striker
Veracruz

ÉLTON
1.59m (5ft 2½in)
Brazil: Midfielder
Al-Qadisiyah

MADSON
1.60m (5ft 3in)
Brazil: Midfielder
Al-Khor

SANTI CAZORLA
1.68m (5ft 6in)
Spain: Midfielder
Arsenal

LIONEL MESSI
1.69m (5ft 6½in)
Argentina: Striker
Barcelona

PETER CROUCH
2.01m (6ft 7in)
England: Striker
Stoke City

COSTEL PANTILIMON
2.03m (6ft 8in)
Romania: Goalkeeper
Watford

YANG CHANGPENG
2.05m (6ft 8½in)
China: Striker
Henan Jianye

KRISTOF VAN HOUT
2.08m (6ft 10in)
Belgium: Goalkeeper
Westerlo

2m
(6ft 6¾in)

1.75m
(5ft 9in)

1.5m
(4ft 11in)

1.25m
(4ft 1in)

1m
(3ft 3½in)

0.75m
(2ft 5½in)

0.5m
(1ft 7½in)

0.25m
(10in)

0m

Tallest and shortest at Brazil World Cup 2014

FRASER FORSTER (England)
2.01m (6ft 7in)
LORENZO INSIGNE (Italy)
1.63m (5ft 4in)

TALLEST TEAM: GERMANY
average **1.85m** (6ft 1in)
SHORTEST TEAM: CHILE
average **1.76m** (5ft 9in)

FOOTBALL'S LONGEST WALK

'It was the worst moment of my career,' said former Italian striker Roberto Baggio about skying his penalty kick over the bar against Brazil in the 1994 World Cup final. It's a cruel way to decide a match, but the penalty shoot-out has provided high drama, along with misery and elation, since it was first introduced to the world's greatest tournament in 1978.

8 July 1982

First shoot-out, West Germany beating France in semifinal 5-4

82 %

of the last 11 shoot-outs, up to and including 2014, have been won by the team taking the first spot kick

1978

The year shoot-outs were introduced, although none were required in the 1978 Argentina tournament

ROBERTO BAGGIO ITALY

WORLD CUP SHOOT-OUT TOTALS

240 penalties taken (170 scored, 70 saved or missed)

53 left foot   **187** right foot

5 out of 13

European teams that have won shoot-outs against a country from another continent

2

The World Cup finals decided on penalties: 1994 and 2006

WORLD CUP SHOOT-OUT WINNERS

	'78	'82	'86	'90	'94	'98	'02	'06	'10	'14
GERMANY		⚽	⚽	⚽				⚽		
ARGENTINA				⚽⚽*		⚽				⚽
FRANCE			⚽			⚽				
BRAZIL					⚽	⚽				⚽
BELGIUM			⚽							
REP. IRELAND				⚽						
BULGARIA					⚽					
SWEDEN					⚽					
SOUTH KOREA							⚽			
SPAIN							⚽			
ITALY								⚽		
PORTUGAL								⚽		
UKRAINE								⚽		
PARAGUAY									⚽	
URUGUAY									⚽	
COSTA RICA										⚽
NETHERLANDS										⚽

* 2 shoot-outs in the same tournament

4

Most shoot-outs won: Germany and Argentina

DEFEATED IN TWO OR MORE SHOOT-OUTS

	'78	'82	'86	'90	'94	'98	'02	'06	'10	'14
ITALY				⚽	⚽	⚽				
ENGLAND				⚽		⚽		⚽		
FRANCE		⚽						⚽		
MEXICO			⚽		⚽					
SPAIN			⚽				⚽			
ROMANIA				⚽	⚽					
NETHERLANDS						⚽				⚽

Switzerland

The only country to miss every penalty in a shoot-out (0–3 v Ukraine in 2006)

RAKING IT IN

Yes, football may be sport but it's also big business, and it doesn't come much bigger than this – the top 20 richest clubs in the world. While selling tickets is important, it's broadcasting, commercial and brand revenue that puts these giants in a different league.

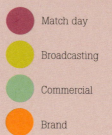

- Match day
- Broadcasting
- Commercial
- Brand

1. REAL MADRID
Team value **3,263**
Revenue **746**

464 | 608
1,100 | 1,091

2. BARCELONA
Team value **3,163**
Revenue **657**

437 | 686
970 | 1,070

3. MANCHESTER UTD
Team value **3,104**
Revenue **703**

446 | 697
1,085 | 875

4. BAYERN MUNICH
Team value **2,347**
Revenue **661**

375 | 381
467
1,124

5. MANCHESTER CITY
Team value **1,375**
Revenue **562**

203 | 170
526 | 476

6. CHELSEA
Team value **1,370**
Revenue **526**

185 | 270
383 | 532

7. ARSENAL
Team value **1,307**
Revenue **487**

164 | 392
268
482

8. LIVERPOOL
Team value **982**
Revenue **415**

138 | 176
319 | 349

9. JUVENTUS
Team value **837**
Revenue **379**

109 | 111
204
414

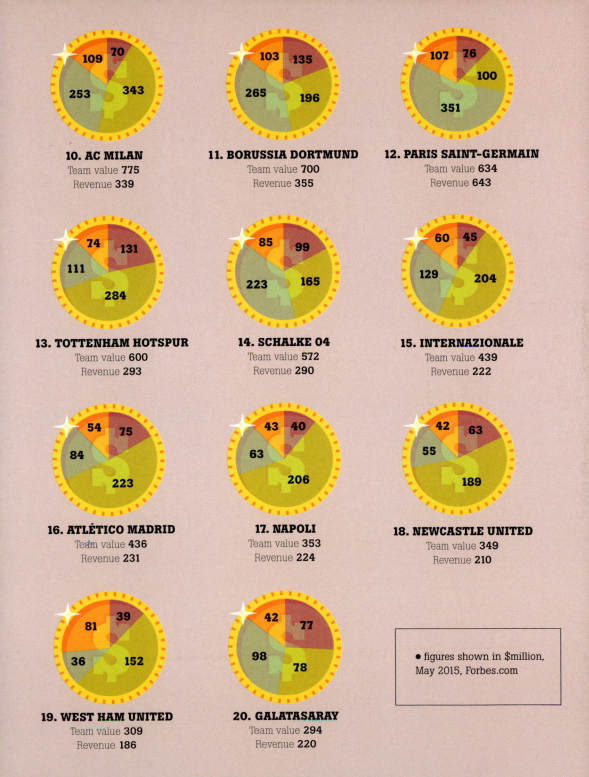

10. AC MILAN
Team value **775**
Revenue **339**

11. BORUSSIA DORTMUND
Team value **700**
Revenue **355**

12. PARIS SAINT-GERMAIN
Team value **634**
Revenue **643**

13. TOTTENHAM HOTSPUR
Team value **600**
Revenue **293**

14. SCHALKE 04
Team value **572**
Revenue **290**

15. INTERNAZIONALE
Team value **439**
Revenue **222**

16. ATLÉTICO MADRID
Team value **436**
Revenue **231**

17. NAPOLI
Team value **353**
Revenue **224**

18. NEWCASTLE UNITED
Team value **349**
Revenue **210**

19. WEST HAM UNITED
Team value **309**
Revenue **186**

20. GALATASARAY
Team value **294**
Revenue **220**

● figures shown in $million,
May 2015, Forbes.com

GIANTS OF EUROPE

All European fans will think their club is a giant. There are teams, though, whose wealth, trophy-winning achievements and fervent support – local and global – lift them just that little bit higher.

*includes Champions League
†includes UEFA Cup

1

CELTIC
Founded 1887

★

League titles **47**
Scottish Cup **36**
European Cup **1**

2

MANCHESTER UNITED
Founded 1878

★

League titles **20**
FA Cup **12**
European Cup* **3**
UEFA Cup Winners' Cup **1**

3

MANCHESTER CITY
Founded 1880

★

League titles **4**
FA Cup **5**
UEFA Cup Winners' Cup **1**

4

LIVERPOOL
Founded 1892

★

League titles **18**
FA Cup **7**
European Cup* **5**
UEFA Cup **3**

5

ARSENAL
Founded 1886

★

League titles **13**
FA Cup **12**
UEFA Cup Winners' Cup **1**

6

CHELSEA
Founded 1905

★

League titles **5**
FA Cup **7**
Champions League **1**
UEFA Europa League **1**
UEFA Cup Winners' Cup **2**

7

PARIS SAINT-GERMAIN
Founded 1970

★

League titles **6**
Coupe de France **10**
UEFA Cup Winners' Cup **1**

8

OLYMPIQUE DE MARSEILLE
Founded 1899

★

League titles **9**
Coupe de France **10**
Champions League **1**

9

AJAX
Founded 1900

★

League titles **33**
KNVB Cup **18**
European Cup* **4**
UEFA Cup **1**
UEFA Cup Winners' Cup **1**

10

PSV EINDHOVEN
Founded 1913

★

League titles **23**
KNVB Cup **9**
European Cup **1**
UEFA Cup **1**

11

BENFICA
Founded 1904

★

League titles **35**
Portuguese Cup **25**
European Cup **2**

12

FC PORTO
Founded 1893

★

League titles **27**
Portuguese Cup **16**
European Cup* **2**
UEFA Europa League† **2**

13

BAYERN MUNICH
Founded 1900
★
League titles **26**
DFB-Pokal **18**
European Cup* **5**
UEFA Cup **1**
UEFA Cup Winners'
Cup **1**

14

BORUSSIA DORTMUND
Founded 1909
★
League titles **8**
DFB-Pokal **3**
Champions League **1**
UEFA Cup Winners'
Cup **1**

15

SCHALKE 04
Founded 1904
★
League titles **7**
DFB-Pokal **5**
UEFA Cup **1**

16

BARCELONA
Founded 1899
★
League titles **24**
Copa del Rey **28**
European Cup* **11**
UEFA Cup Winners'
Cup **4**

17

REAL MADRID
Founded 1902
★
League titles **32**
Copa del Rey **19**
European Cup* **11**
UEFA Cup **2**

18

ATLÉTICO MADRID
Founded 1903
★
League titles **10**
Copa del Rey **10**
UEFA Europa League **2**
UEFA Cup Winners'
Cup **1**

19

AC MILAN
Founded 1899
★
League titles **18**
Coppa Italia **5**
European Cup* **7**
UEFA Cup Winners'
Cup **2**

20

INTERNAZIONALE
Founded 1908
★
League titles **18**
Coppa Italia **7**
European Cup* **3**
UEFA Cup **3**

21

JUVENTUS
Founded 1897
★
League titles **32**
Coppa Italia **11**
European Cup* **2**
UEFA Cup **3**
UEFA Cup Winners'
Cup **1**

22

GALATASARAY SK
Founded 1905
★
League titles **20**
Turkish Cup **17**
UEFA Cup **1**

45

I'M SORRY, WHAT DID YOU SAY YOUR NAME WAS?

Pity the poor kit makers who have to deal with the weird, wide and wonderful names that grace the game. Some footballers and clubs opt for a shorter version, others embrace the full glory of their moniker, while much can get lost in translation.

THE SHORT

THE LONG

JOÃO ALVES DE ASSIS SILVA
CORINTHIANS & BRAZIL
His full name is actually one of the longest in football.

DEMBA BA
SHANGHAI SHENHUA & SENEGAL
Names don't come much shorter, making a nice simple job for the shirt printer.

SOKRATIS PAPASTATHOPOULOS
BORUSSIA DORTMUND & GREECE
A surname so long that the Greek player is on first-name terms only.

THE VERY LONG

Clwb Pel Droed Llanfairpwllgwyngyllg

Nooit Opgeven Altijd Doorzetten Aangenaam Door Vermaak En Nuttig Door Ontspanning Combinatie Breda

Netherlands, Eerste Divisie [86 letters] • thankfully, shortened to NAC Breda

THE STRANGE

CREEDENCE CLEARWATER COUTO
Clearly, Creedence's parents were big US music fans; his teammates at Santa Cruz (Brazil) call him 'Paulista'

CHRIST BONGO
Congo Republic, 4 caps (2000–01)

NORMAN CONQUEST
Australia, 11 caps (1947–50)

MARK DE MAN
Belgium, 5 caps (2007–08) – and yes, he is a defensive player

JAN VENNEGOOR OF HESSELINK
NETHERLANDS, RETIRED
'Of' in Dutch means 'or' – so this footballing mouthful dates back to two indecisive farming families who combined their names on marriage.

ALEX OXLADE-CHAMBERLAIN
ARSENAL & ENGLAND
The 'Ox', for short, opts just for Chamberlain on his shirt to avoid a double-barrelled letter barrage.

BASTIAN SCHWEINSTEIGER
CHICAGO FIRE & GERMANY
Great fun to say, but also a surname with one of the more peculiar of meanings: 'pig climber'.

erychwyrndrobwllllantysiliogogogoch
Welsh Alliance League [70 letters] • known, more succinctly, as CPD Llanfairpwll

Borussia Verein für Leibesübungen 1900 Mönchengladbach e.V.
Bundesliga, Germany [53 characters] • the team's nickname, 'The Foals', makes life easier for the fans

A CLEAN PAIR OF HEELS

Whoosh! Defenders hate sheer speed. Only 5 km/h (3.1 mph) separates the average top speeds of the 10 fastest footballers*, but that can easily mean the difference between a last-ditch tackle and even the paciest fullback left for dead. But can footballers hold their own against other athletes – or a hare?

(*based on FIFA study, published in *Mundo Deportivo* newspaper, 2014)

10
ALEXIS SÁNCHEZ
Arsenal/Chile
30.1 km/h (18.7 mph)

9
ARJEN ROBBEN
Bayern Munich/
Netherlands
30.4 km/h (18.9 mph)

8
FRANCK RIBÉRY
Bayern Munich/France
30.7 km/h (19 mph)

DRI ARCHER
American Football
running back/USA
30.9 km/h (19.2 mph)

**GIANT
TORTOISE**
0.3 km/h
(0.19 mph)

7
WAYNE ROONEY
Manchester
United/England
31.2 km/h (19.4 mph)

6
LIONEL MESSI
Barcelona/Argentina
32.5 km/h (20.2 mph)

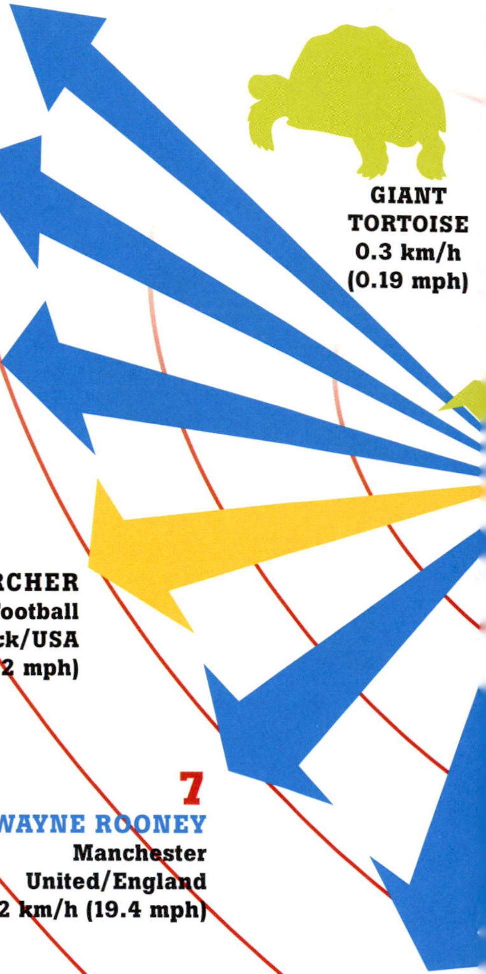

BOLTS FROM THE BLUE

37 km/h (23 mph)
ARJEN ROBBEN
Bayern Munich/Netherlands
Fastest ever recorded single
football sprint: World Cup,
Netherlands v Spain, 13 June 2014

PIERRE-EMERICK AUBAMEYANG
Borussia Dortmund/Gabon
Covered 30m (32yd) in 3.7 seconds at a
pre-season training camp in 2013 – 0.08
seconds faster than Usain Bolt when he
recorded his 100m world record

CHEETAH
93.3 km/h (58 mph)

FLORENT MANAUDOU
Swimmer/
France (50m freestyle world record 20.26 secs) 8.9 km/h (5.5 mph)

BROWN HARE
72.4 km/h (45 mph)

USAIN BOLT
Athlete/Jamaica
(100m world record 9.58 secs)
32.6 km/h (23.4 mph)

1
ANTONIO VALENCIA
Manchester United/Ecuador
35.1 km/h (21.9 mph)

2
GARETH BALE
Real Madrid/Wales
34.7 km/h (21.6 mph)

3
AARON LENNON
Everton/England
33.8 km/h
(21 mph)

5
THEO WALCOTT
senal/England
32.7 km/h
(20.3 mph)

4
CRISTIANO RONALDO
Real Madrid/
Portugal 33.6 km/h
(20.9 mph)

WORLD CUP WIZARDS

These are the top 22 brilliant goal scorers who have lit up 20 World Cups, from Uruguay in 1930 to Brazil in 2014. Many have also been winners of the Golden Shoe, or Boot – awarded by FIFA for the most goals scored in an individual Word Cup tournament. Legends, all.

22 TOP GOAL SCORERS AT THE WORLD CUP

	NAME	COUNTRY	TOURNAMENTS	MATCHES PLAYED	GOALS SCORED
1	MIROSLAV KLOSE	Germany	2002, 2006, 2010, 2014	24	16
2	RONALDO	Brazil	1994, 1998, 2002, 2006	19	15
3	GERD MÜLLER	West Germany	1970, 1974	13	14
4	JUST FONTAINE	France	1958	6	13
5	PELÉ	Brazil	1958, 1962, 1966, 1970	14	12
= 6	SÁNDOR KOCSIS	Hungary	1954	5	11
=	JÜRGEN KLINSMANN	Germany	1990, 1994, 1998	17	11
= 8	HELMUT RAHN	West Germany	1954, 1958	10	10
=	TEÓFILO CUBILLAS	Peru	1970, 1978, 1982	13	10
=	GRZEGORZ LATO	Poland	1974, 1978, 1982	20	10
=	GARY LINEKER	England	1986, 1990	12	10
=	GABRIEL BATISTUTA	Argentina	1994, 1998, 2002	12	10
=	THOMAS MÜLLER	Germany	2010, 2014	13	10
= 14	VAVÁ	Brazil	1958, 1962	10	9
=	UWE SEELER	West Germany	1958, 1962, 1966, 1970	21	9
=	EUSÉBIO	Portugal	1966	6	9
=	JAIRZINHO	Brazil	1966, 1970, 1974	16	9
=	PAOLO ROSSI	Italy	1978, 1982, 1986	14	9
=	KARL-HEINZ RUMMENIGGE	West Germany	1978, 1982, 1986	19	9
=	ROBERTO BAGGIO	Italy	1990, 1994, 1998	16	9
=	CHRISTIAN VIERI	Italy	1998, 2002	9	9
=	DAVID VILLA	Spain	2006, 2010, 2014	12	9

GOLDEN BOOT WINNERS

The World Cup top scorer has received an award only since 1982,
first as the Golden Shoe, then, since 2010, the Golden Boot.

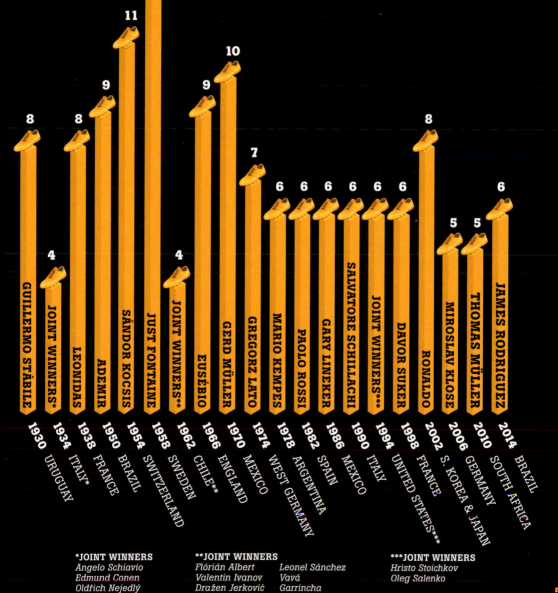

Goals	Player	Year	Country
8	GUILLERMO STÁBILE	1930	URUGUAY
4	JOINT WINNERS*	1934	ITALY*
8	LEONIDAS	1938	FRANCE
9	ADEMIR	1950	BRAZIL
11	SÁNDOR KOCSIS	1954	SWITZERLAND
13	JUST FONTAINE	1958	SWEDEN
4	JOINT WINNERS**	1962	CHILE**
9	EUSÉBIO	1966	ENGLAND
10	GERD MÜLLER	1970	MEXICO
7	GREGORZ LATO	1974	WEST GERMANY
6	MARIO KEMPES	1978	ARGENTINA
6	PAOLO ROSSI	1982	SPAIN
6	GARY LINEKER	1986	MEXICO
6	SALVATORE SCHILLACI	1990	ITALY
6	JOINT WINNERS***	1994	UNITED STATES***
6	DAVOR SUKER	1998	FRANCE
8	RONALDO	2002	S. KOREA & JAPAN
5	MIROSLAV KLOSE	2006	GERMANY
5	THOMAS MÜLLER	2010	SOUTH AFRICA
6	JAMES RODRIGUEZ	2014	BRAZIL

*JOINT WINNERS
Angelo Schiavio
Edmund Conen
Oldřich Nejedlý

**JOINT WINNERS
Flórián Albert   *Leonel Sánchez*
Valentin Ivanov   *Vavá*
Dražen Jerković   *Garrincha*

***JOINT WINNERS
Hristo Stoichkov
Oleg Salenko

STRICTLY LATIN

Yes, it's soccer samba tango time, as the countries of South America battle it out in the oldest international football competition – the Copa América. It began in 1916 as the Campeonato Sud Americano de Football (South American Football Championship), took on its present title in 1975 and has been fuelling continental rivalries ever since.

[★ = tournament winner]

COPA AMÉRICA

1975 No fixed host
★ Peru
Runner-up: Colombia
0–1/2–1 play-off: 1–0

1979 No fixed host
★ Paraguay
Runner-up: Chile
3–0/0–1 playoff: 0–0
(Paraguay won 3–1 on aggregate)

1983 No fixed host
★ Uruguay
Runner-up: Brazil
2–0/1–1 *(Uruguay won on points)*

1987 ARGENTINA
★ Uruguay
Runner-up: Chile
1–0

1989 BRAZIL
★ Brazil
Runner-up: Uruguay
Brazil won all 3 games in round-robin final group against Uruguay, Argentina and Paraguay

1991 CHILE
★ Argentina
Runner-up: Brazil
Argentina won 2 and drew 1 against Brazil, Colombia and Chile in a round-robin final group

1993 ECUADOR
★ Argentina
Runner-up: Mexico
2–1

1995 URUGUAY
★ Uruguay
Runner-up: Brazil
1–1 *(5–3 on penalties)*

1997 BOLIVIA
★ Brazil
Runner-up: Bolivia
3–1

1999 PARAGUAY
★ Brazil
Runner-up: Uruguay
3–0

2001 COLOMBIA
★ Colombia
Runner-up: Mexico
1–0

2004 PERU
★ Brazil
Runner-up: Argentina
2–2 *(4–2 on penalties)*

2007 VENEZUELA
★ Brazil
Runner-up: Argentina
3–0

2011 ARGENTINA
★ Uruguay
Runner-up: Paraguay
3–0

2015 CHILE
★ Chile
Runner-up: Argentina
0–0 *(4–1 on penalties)*

BIGGEST VICTORY

Argentina 12–0 Ecuador
(1942)

CAMPEONATO SUD AMERICANO DE FOOTBALL (South American Football Championship) tournament winners

1916 Uruguay		**1939** Peru	
1917 Uruguay		**1941** Argentina	
1919 Brazil		**1942** Uruguay	
1920 Uruguay		**1945** Argentina	
1921 Argentina		**1946** Argentina	
1922 Brazil		**1947** Argentina	
1923 Uruguay		**1949** Brazil	
1924 Uruguay		**1953** Paraguay	
1925 Argentina		**1955** Argentina	
1926 Uruguay		**1956** Uruguay	
1927 Argentina		**1957** Argentina	
1929 Argentina		**1959** Argentina	
1935 Uruguay		**1963** Bolivia	
1937 Argentina		**1967** Uruguay	

no tournament 1968–74

Tournament wins 1916–2015

15 Uruguay
14 Argentina
8 Brazil
2 Paraguay
2 Peru
1 Chile
1 Colombia
1 Bolivia

6 The number of nations outside of South America that have been invited to join the tournament since 1993:

Costa Rica *(1997, 2001, 2004, 2011)*
Honduras *(2001)*
Jamaica *(2015)*
Japan *(1999)*
Mexico *(1993, 1995, 1997, 1999, 2001, 2004, 2007, 2011, 2015)*
USA *(1993, 1995, 2007)*

TOP GOALSCORERS

17 **Norberto Méndez** *(1945–56), Argentina*
17 **Zizinho** *(1942–57), Brazil*

15 **Teodoro Fernández** *(1935–47), Peru*
15 **Severino Varela** *(1935–42), Uruguay*

13 **Ademir** *(1945–53), Brazil*
13 **Gabriel Batistuta** *(1991–2002), Argentina*
13 **Jairzinho** *(1964–82), Brazil*
13 **José Manuel Moreno** *(1936–50), Argentina*
13 **Héctor Scarone** *(1917–32), Uruguay*

12 **Roberto Porta** *(1937–45), Uruguay*
12 **Ángel Romano** *(1911–27), Uruguay*

11 **Víctor Agustín Ugarte** *(1947–63), Bolivia*
11 **Herminio Masantonio** *(1935–42), Argentina*

BUSTING THE BUDGET

In the past one hundred or so years football transfer fees have spiralled from sums you could easily slip into a small brown envelope to amounts that probably would not fit into an articulated lorry. It started with £100 changing hands in the Midlands of England in 1893 and peaked with Paul Pogba's move for £89.3 million to Manchester United in 2016. Where will it all end?

TREVOR FRANCIS

is often thought to have been the first £1 million footballer for his transfer from Birmingham City to Nottingham Forest – in fact, the fee was £950,000, which rose to £1.18 million only with the addition of VAT and various other levies.

DIEGO MARADONA

is the only player to break the world transfer record twice. Barcelona snapped him up for £3 million in 1982 then sold him to Napoli for £5 million in 1984.

£100	1893	**WILLIE GROVES** (Scotland) West Bromwich Albion to Aston Villa
£1,000	1905	**ALF COMMON** (England) Sunderland to Middlesbrough
£5,000	1922	**SYD PUDDEFOOT** (England) West Ham Utd to Falkirk
£10,890	1928	**DAVID JACK** (England) Bolton Wanderers to Arsenal
£23,000	1932	**BERNABÉ FERREYRA** (Argentina) Tigre to River Plate
£52,000	1952	**HANS JEPPSON** (Sweden) Atalanta to Napoli
£72,000	1954	**JUAN SCHIAFFINO** (Uruguay) Peñarol to AC Milan
£152,000	1961	**LUIS SUÁREZ** (Spain) Barcelona to Internazionale
£250,000	1963	**ANGELO SORMANI** (Italy) Mantova to AS Roma
£300,000	1967	**HARALD NIELSEN** (Denmark) Bologna to Internazionale
£500,000	1968	**PIETRO ANASTASI** (Italy) Varese to Juventus
£922,000	1973	**JOHAN CRUYFF** (Netherlands) Ajax to Barcelona
£1,200,000	1975	**GIUSEPPE SAVOLDI** (Italy) Bologna to Napoli
£1,750,000	1976	**PAOLO ROSSI** (Italy) Juventus to Vicenza
£3,000,000	1982	**DIEGO MARADONA** (Argentina) Boca Juniors to Barcelona
£5,000,000	1984	**DIEGO MARADONA** (Argentina) Barcelona to Napoli

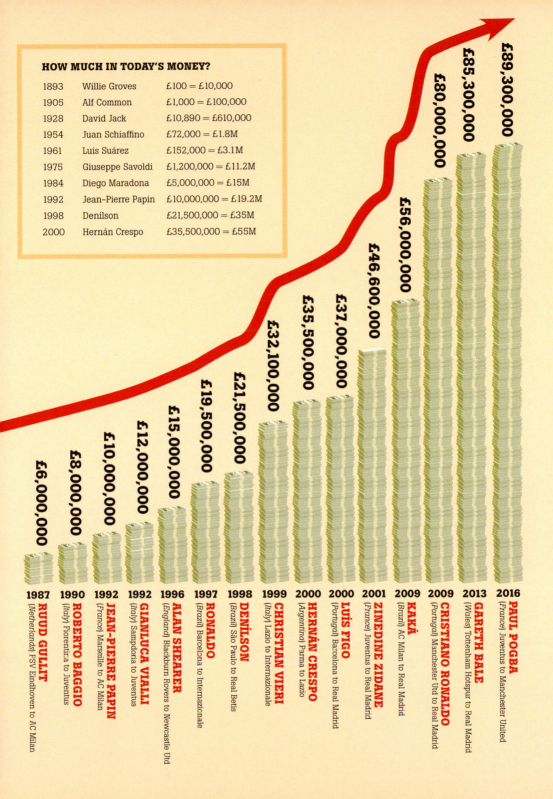

HOW MUCH IN TODAY'S MONEY?

1893	Willie Groves	£100 = £10,000
1905	Alf Common	£1,000 = £100,000
1928	David Jack	£10,890 = £610,000
1954	Juan Schiaffino	£72,000 = £1.8M
1961	Luis Suárez	£152,000 = £3.1M
1975	Giuseppe Savoldi	£1,200,000 = £11.2M
1984	Diego Maradona	£5,000,000 = £15M
1992	Jean-Pierre Papin	£10,000,000 = £19.2M
1998	Denílson	£21,500,000 = £35M
2000	Hernán Crespo	£35,500,000 = £55M

£6,000,000
£8,000,000
£10,000,000
£12,000,000
£15,000,000
£19,500,000
£21,500,000
£32,100,000
£35,500,000
£37,000,000
£46,600,000
£56,000,000
£80,000,000
£85,300,000
£89,300,000

1987
RUUD GULLIT
(Netherlands) PSV Eindhoven to AC Milan

1990
ROBERTO BAGGIO
(Italy) Fiorentina to Juventus

1992
JEAN-PIERRE PAPIN
(France) Marseille to AC Milan

1992
GIANLUCA VIALLI
(Italy) Sampdoria to Juventus

1996
ALAN SHEARER
(England) Blackburn Rovers to Newcastle Utd

1997
RONALDO
(Brazil) Barcelona to Internazionale

1998
DENÍLSON
(Brazil) São Paulo to Real Betis

1999
CHRISTIAN VIERI
(Italy) Lazio to Internazionale

2000
HERNÁN CRESPO
(Argentina) Parma to Lazio

2000
LUÍS FIGO
(Portugal) Barcelona to Real Madrid

2001
ZINEDINE ZIDANE
(France) Juventus to Real Madrid

2009
KAKÁ
(Brazil) AC Milan to Real Madrid

2009
CRISTIANO RONALDO
(Portugal) Manchester Utd to Real Madrid

2013
GARETH BALE
(Wales) Tottenham Hotspur to Real Madrid

2016
PAUL POGBA
(France) Juventus to Manchester United

A HEAD OF THE GAME

Footballers like to think they are dedicated followers of fashion, and that extends to their hairstyles. But they can be a vain, ill-advised bunch and make strange, and downright appalling, hair choices. There are even those who are remembered more for their hairdo than what they did on the pitch. Pick a winner from this big league of coiffured calamities.

RUDI VÖLLER
Germany 1982–94

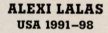

ALEXI LALAS
USA 1991–98

MARIO BALOTELLI
Italy 2010–

STEFAN EFFENBERG
Germany 1991–98

RUUD GULLIT
Netherlands 1981–94

ROBERTO BAGGIO
Italy 1988–2004

BOBBY CHARLTON
England 1958–70

MAROUANE FELLAINI
Belgium 2007–

CHRIS WADDLE
England 1985–91

ABEL XAVIER
Portugal 1993–2002

← **CARLOS VALDERRAMA**
Columbia 1985–98

The flamboyant midfielder known as *El Pibe*
('The Kid') took his mane of curly blond locks
to three World Cups and played 111 times for
his country, scoring 11 goals.

GAFFER GREATS

It's about 11 players performing on the pitch. But it's also about the man in the dugout, screaming instructions as his blood pressure soars. Behind the finest teams is a manager who, through the alchemy of tactical nous, motivation, respect – even love and fear – gets a disparate bunch of footballers to reach the heights of the game. Debate about the greatest 'gaffers' is endless, but here are some of the best.

SIR ALEX FERGUSON Scotland, 1941–

16 league titles · Aberdeen, Manchester United
2 UEFA Cup Winners' Cup · Aberdeen, Manchester United
2 Champions League · Manchester United
1 FIFA Club World Cup · Manchester United

Add 14 domestic cups in Scotland and England and Ferguson becomes the greatest trophy-winning manager ever. Along with Trapattoni, he has won more European trophies than any other manager.

UDO LATTEK Germany, 1935–2015

8 league titles · Bayern Munich, Borussia Mönchengladbach
1 European Cup · Bayern Munich
1 UEFA Cup · Borussia Mönchengladbach
1 UEFA Cup Winners' Cup · Barcelona

Lattek achieved his impressive haul of trophies by the time he retired early, at 52 – and having never been a professional player. He is one of only two managers (Trapattoni the other) to have won all three major European club competitions.

BOB PAISLEY England, 1919–96

6 league titles · Liverpool
3 European Cup · Liverpool
1 UEFA Cup · Liverpool
1 UEFA Super Cup · Liverpool

No one has surpassed Paisley for sheer devotion to one club. The softly spoken Englishman spent 44 years at Liverpool as player, physiotherapist, coach and manager. He oversaw the club's dominance of English football from 1975 to 1983, securing six titles in consecutive seasons. With Carlo Ancelotti, Paisley is still the only manager to have won the European Cup (now the Champions League) three times.

OTTMAR HITZFELD Germany, 1949–

9 league titles · Grasshopper Club Zürich, Borussia Dortmund, Bayern Munich
2 Champions League · Borussia Dortmund, Bayern Munich

Seen by many as the greatest of Bundesliga mangers, Hitzfeld won the league title five times with Bayern, four of those in consecutive seasons from 1999 to 2003. He finished his career by taking Switzerland to the 2014 World Cup.

JOSÉ MOURINHO Portugal, 1963–

8 league titles · FC Porto, Chelsea, Internazionale, Real Madrid
2 Champions League · FC Porto, Internazionale
1 UEFA Cup · FC Porto

Like Lattek, Mourinho achieved eight league titles by the age of 52 – but the fiercely ambitious, ruthlessly efficient and hyper-confident Portuguese surely has more to come. He is one of only five managers to have won the league in four different countries.

WORLD COACH OF THE YEAR

The Best FIFA men's Coach award is decided from a shortlist of 10 by votes from coaches and captains of international teams, sports journalists, and since 2016, football fans.

2016
Claudio Ranieri (Italy, Leicester City)

2015
Luis Enrique (Spain, Barcelona)

2014
Joachim Löw (Germany, national team)

2013
Jupp Heynckes (Germany, Bayern Munich)

2012
Vicente del Bosque (Spain, national team)

2011
Pep Guardiola (Spain, Barcelona)

BRIAN CLOUGH England, 1935–2004

2 league titles · Derby County, Nottingham Forest
2 European Cup · Nottingham Forest
1 UEFA Super Cup · Nottingham Forest

Clough took perennially under-achieving side Nottingham Forest to European Cup glory in 1979 and 1980 – the most unlikely success story in the tournament's history. As a player, Clough was a prolific goalscorer for Middlesbrough and Sunderland, netting 251 times in 274 league appearances, until knee injury ended his career. His dream to manage England never materialized and he lasted only 44 days as manager of Leeds United in 1974. It was arguably Clough's prickly, combative and arrogant nature that stood in the way of true managerial greatness – though not in his own eyes:

> I wouldn't say I was the best manager in the business. But I was in the top one.

GIOVANNI TRAPATTONI Italy, 1939–

10 league titles · Juventus, Internazionale, Bayern Munich, Benfica, Red Bull Salzburg
3 UEFA Cup · Juventus, Internazionale
1 UEFA Cup Winners' Cup · Juventus
1 European Cup · Juventus

League titles spanning 40 years (1977–2007) in four countries with four clubs make Trapattoni one of the most successful managers in Serie A history. He is also the only manager to have won all UEFA European club competitions and the Intercontinental Cup.

ERNST HAPPEL Austria, 1925–92

8 league titles · Feyenoord, Club Brugge, Hamburger SV, FC Swarovski Tirol
2 European Cup · Feyenoord, Hamburger SV

Happel won leagues in four different countries and led Feyenoord and Hamburger SV to their only European Cup victories, becoming the first manager to win the trophy with two different clubs. He also took a hugely talented Netherlands side to the 1978 World Cup final.

RINUS MICHELS Netherlands, 1928–2005

5 league titles · Ajax, Barcelona
1 European Cup · Ajax
1 UEFA European Championship · Netherlands

Michels may not have won as many titles as other greats, but he left an indelible mark on the game with the radical 'total football' he introduced at Ajax. The Netherlands team he took to the final of the 1974 World Cup is often regarded as the best never to have won. Michels made amends in 1988 by leading the Dutch to victory at the European Championship.

MIGUEL MUÑOZ Spain, 1922–1990

9 league titles · Real Madrid
2 European Cup · Real Madrid

As a Real Madrid player, Muñoz won three European Cups (1956–58), two as captain. He then took the club to two European Cup victories (1960 and 1966), becoming the first to win the trophy as a player and a manager. Leadership of Spain proved less fruitful, though Muñoz did lead his country to the 1984 European Championship final, losing to France 2–0.

LION, MEET ARMADILLO

Ever since World Cup Willie strode lion-like onto the mugs, tea towels and T-shirts of England in 1966, every World Cup has had its mascot. There have been some strange, if not downright bizarre, national choices.

1966
ENGLAND
World Cup Willie
(a lion)

1970
MEXICO
Juanito

1974
WEST GERMANY
Tip and Tap

1978
ARGENTINA
Gauchito

1982
SPAIN
Naranjito
(an orange)

1986
MEXICO
Pique
(a pepper)

1990
ITALY
Ciao

1994
USA
Striker
(a dog)

1998
FRANCE
Footix
(a cockerel)

2002
SOUTH KOREA & JAPAN
Ato, Kaz and Nik
(anyone's guess ...)

2006
GERMANY
Goleo VI
(a lion – again)

2010
SOUTH AFRICA
Zakumi
(a leopard)

2014
BRAZIL
Fuleco
(an armadillo)

THE RICH LIST

We all know top professional footballers earn eye-watering amounts of money for kicking a ball around a pitch. The players here have earned more than most but also have that knack – or employ those who have it – of turning millions into ever more millions through sometimes surprising income streams.

LIONEL MESSI earned **65 million euros** in 2014 – equal to around **1.4 million euros** for every league and cup game he played for Barcelona that year

CRISTIANO RONALDO was estimated to earn **$32 million** in 2016 from endorsements for Nike, Tag Heuer and other brands

WAYNE ROONEY had his first winner as a racehorse owner in 2012, when Pippy, a **£63,000** colt, won at Wolverhampton racecourse

	WORTH ($million)	FOOTBALL CONTRACT
DAVID BECKHAM retired	316	
CRISTIANO RONALDO Real Madrid	210	⚽
LIONEL MESSI Barcelona	200	⚽
NEYMAR Barcelona	135	⚽
ZLATAN IBRAHIMOVIĆ Manchester United	105	⚽
WAYNE ROONEY Manchester United	103	⚽
KAKÁ Orlando City	96	⚽
SAMUEL ETO'O Antalyaspor	87	⚽
RAÚL retired	85	
RONALDINHO Barcelona ambassador	83	
FRANK LAMPARD retired	80	
BASTIAN SCHWEINSTEIGER Chicago Fire	75	⚽
RIO FERDINAND retired	72	
GIANLUIGI BUFFON Juventus	68	⚽
STEVEN GERRARD retired	64	

Figures in $million, March 2015, goal.com

ENDORSE-MENTS	PROPERTY DEALS	BUSINESS	WRITING	RACE-HORSES	MODELLING	ACTING	TEAM OWNER
✓	🏠	🤝			🧑	🎬	🏆
✓	🏠	🤝			🧑		
✓	🏠	🤝					
✓					🧑		
✓	🏠	🤝	✏️				
✓	🏠			🐎			
✓	🏠						
✓							
✓	🏠	🤝					
✓							
✓	🏠		✏️				
✓							
✓	🏠	🤝	✏️				
✓		🤝					
✓	🏠						

DAVID BECKHAM has his own Miami MLS franchise, bought at a discount (as negotiated in his 2007 contract with LA Galaxy) for **$25 million**

FRANK LAMPARD has so far authored **17** children's books about the footballing adventures of a little boy called – unsurprsingly – Frankie and his 'magic football'

BEFORE THEY WERE FAMOUS

Many youngsters grow up wanting to be a footballer. While some realize their dream, there are those who decide to become a sweary chef, an existentialist novelist or even Christ's representative on Earth. A surprising number of celebs have shown footballing promise – but why all the goalies?

ROD STEWART
ROCK STAR
1945–
Gravel-voiced singer with the Jeff Beck Group and the Faces, and mega solo artist, Stewart had a trial as a teenager with London club Brentford. He never got the follow-up call.

NIELS BOHR
PHYSICIST
1885–1962
Nobel Prize-winning Danish physicist, and goalkeeper, Niels donned the gloves for Copenhagen team Akademisk Boldklub. His younger brother, and future maths genius, Harald, won a silver medal at the 1908 Olympics playing for Denmark.

GORDON RAMSAY
CHEF & RESTAURATEUR
1966–
The F-ing celebrity chef took to cooking once his hopes of a football career ended with cruciate ligament damage. He had a trial in two exhibition matches for the Scottish club Rangers but, contrary to some claims, never played for the first team – or the reserves.

JULIO IGLESIAS
CROONER
1943–
A car crash in the early 1960s put paid to the future Spanish balladeer's fledgling career as a promising goalkeeper in the Real Madrid youth team. A guitar given to him to aid recuperation sealed the young Julio's fate.

LUCIANO PAVAROTTI
OPERA SINGER
1935–2007
The great Italian operatic tenor was, in younger – and slimmer – days, a passionate footballer, playing as goalkeeper then winger in the youth team of Modena, his home town.

SEAN CONNERY
ACTOR
1930–
While appearing in the musical *South Pacific*, the 23-year-old future James Bond was offered a contract and £25-a-week by Matt Busby, manager of Manchester United. Sean, who had also been offered a trial with the Scottish side East Fife, turned Busby down. Smart move, 007 …

STEVE HARRIS
ROCK STAR
1956–

Bassist for, and founder member of, heavy metal band Iron Maiden, Harris grew up, like David Beckham, in Leytonstone, East London. His football skills were spotted by scout Wally St Pier (discoverer of Bobby Moore, Geoff Hurst and Frank Lampard, among many) and trained with West Ham United. The lure of head-banging rock, though, proved too much.

DAVID FROST
TV PRESENTER
1939–2013

The future 1960s satirist, inquisitor of politicians and talk-show host turned down a contract with Nottingham Forest to go to Cambridge University. A Forest scout had spotted Frost scoring eight goals from eight shots in a school match.

KAREL WOJTYLA –
aka POPE JOHN PAUL II
POPE
1920–2005

Karel played in goal for his school team in the Polish town of Wadowice, and then at university in Kraków, impressing onlookers with his powerful build. He later became a Catholic priest and the first Polish pope.

ALBERT CAMUS
AUTHOR
1913–60

A bout of TB ended the footballing days of the Nobel Prize-winning French author of *L'Étranger* (*The Stranger*). Albert had been goalkeeper for the Racing Universitaire Algérois (RUA) junior team. When asked whether he preferred football or the theatre, Camus replied, 'Football, without hesitation.'

ARTHUR CONAN DOYLE
AUTHOR
1859–1930

Elementary it isn't to imagine the creator of Sherlock Holmes taking to the football pitch in long shorts and jumper. And yet, the athletic Conan Doyle, under the pseudonym A.C. Smith, played as a (yes, you've guessed it) goalkeeper for amateur side Portsmouth AFC.

VIRTUAL FANS

Thanks to social media, these days you don't need to live in the same town, country or even continent to follow the ups and downs of your favourite football team. Remarkably, the Twitter followers of Premier League clubs have been mapped, with some surprisingly far–flung affiliations. Witness the global spread for the four clubs with the most widespread followings.

🔴 **Manchester United** (10.3 m followers)

🟡 **Arsenal** (9.3 m)

🔵 **Chelsea** (8.1 m)

🟢 **Liverpool** (6.9 m)

February 2017 figures

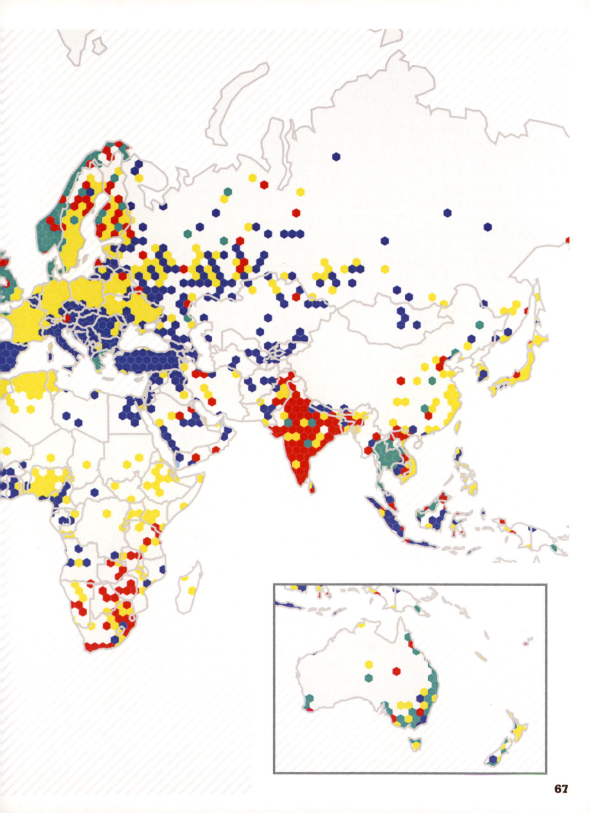

PERFECT PAIRS

Astaire and Rogers, Lennon and McCartney, Holmes and Watson – to those perfect pairs you can add the likes of Xavi and Iniesta, Henry and Bergkamp, Gullit and Van Basten. Now and then, football has produced partnerships, in defence, midfield or attack, that were matches made in heaven. As with all couples, favourites vary, but here are twosomes that would entertain at any football party.

JOHAN NEESKENS & JOHAN CRUYFF
Ajax, Barcelona and Netherlands

Without Neeskens commanding the centre of midfield, for club and country, Cruyff would never have been able to express his skills as gloriously as he did. Together they won three consecutive European Cups (1971–73) with Ajax and took the Netherlands to the 1974 World Cup final.

EMILIO BUTRAGUEÑO & HUGO SÁNCHEZ
Real Madrid

They didn't get on, but as an attacking duo the Spaniard and Mexican fired Real Madrid to five consecutive La Ligas from 1985–86 to 1989–90, when Sánchez scored 38 goals in 35 games, each with just one touch. Butragueño scored 123 goals in 341 league appearances for Real.

JOHN TOSHACK & KEVIN KEEGAN
Liverpool

A big man and little man combination, nicknamed 'Batman and Robin', that worked wonders for Liverpool in their 1970s heyday. The uncanny understanding between the two helped the Merseysiders to three league titles and two UEFA Cups. The pair scored 196 goals for the Reds.

RUUD GULLIT & MARCO VAN BASTEN
AC Milan, Netherlands

Midfielder Gullit and striker Van Basten formed the attacking spine of the great AC Milan side of the late 1980s. They took Milan to the Serie A title in 1987–88 and followed this up with two European Cups in 1988–89 and 1989–90. The pair also scored the two goals that won the 1988 European Championship for the Netherlands.

GEORGE BEST & DENIS LAW
Manchester United

Best possibly the most stylish player of all time, Law simply a goal machine – together, a manager's dream. Both men

XAVI & INIESTA
Barcelona and Spain

The two little midfield masters, and supreme exponents of the tika-taka short-passing style of football, first came together in the 2002–03 season at Barcelona, though it wasn't until 2004–05 that the partnership took off. They

played for 11 years at United, mostly together, with Best scoring 179, often spectacular, goals in 470 games and Law burying an amazing 237 chances in 404 appearances.

FERENC PUSKÁS & ALFREDO DI STÉFANO
Real Madrid

Greatest of the lot? The Argentinian, later Spanish, Di Stéfano scored 165 goals over five seasons (1956–60) in which Real Madrid won consecutive European Cups. He was joined in 1958 by Puskás to make a formidable strikeforce. Within a few months they both scored hat-tricks in a 10–1 demolition of Las Palmas. Puskás went on to score 242 goals in 262 appearances for Real.

box-to-box driving force. Vieira provided the assist for Petit's goal in the 1998 World Cup final, and the pair steered France to victory at the 2000 European Championship.

RAÚL
& FERNANDO MORIENTES
Real Madrid and Spain

One of a seemingly endless procession of great Real Madrid striking partnerships, Raúl and Morientes scored more than 200 goals in a golden five years between 1997 and 2002, helping the club to two La Liga titles and three Champions Leagues. They were mainstays of the Spanish team, too, with 102 and 47 caps respectively.

THIERRY HENRY
& DENNIS BERGKAMP
Arsenal

Two cooler frontline customers you could not hope to meet, and both integral to Arsenal's unbeaten 2003–04 'Invincibles' season. Henry was the more prolific goalscorer, netting 228 times for Arsenal, but a high proportion of those would never have happened without Berkgamp's prodigious 94 assists.

RYAN GIGGS
& DAVID BECKHAM
Manchester United

You could add Roy Keane and Paul Scholes to complete the fearsome foursome that spearheaded United's treble-hunt in 1999. But the glamour points go to the mesmerizing defender-beating skills of Giggs on the left and the crossing and dead-ball brilliance of Beckham on the right.

ROBERTO CARLOS
& CAFU
Brazil

An awesome pairing, Carlos and Cafu reinvented the full-back role, giving it an attacking thrust rarely seen before. Their powerful, surging runs down the wing, plus the stinging shots of Carlos, did much to bring Brazil the World Cup in 2002. Their joint tally of caps – 267.

ALESSANDRO COSTACURTA
& PAOLO MALDINI
AC Milan and Italy

Both one-club men, with 458 and 647 league appearances under the belt, who were still playing for Milan aged 41, these two granite-like defenders shared seven Serie A titles and five European Cup or Champions League triumphs. Between them they notched up 185 caps for Italy as well.

won the first of seven La Liga titles that season, which the two Spaniards followed up with four Champions League trophies, two UEFA Super Cups and two FIFA Club World Cups. Playing for Spain they shared the 2010 World Cup and the 2008 and 2012 European Championship.

RUDI VÖLLER
& JÜRGEN KLINSMANN
West Germany

Never together at club level, the two Germans nevertheless formed an irresistible striking force at the 1990 World Cup, both scoring three times on the way to the final. Each man scored an impressive 47 goals for his country and they collectively won 198 caps.

EMMANUEL PETIT
& PATRICK VIEIRA
Arsenal and France

Although they won only one title together with Arsenal (1997–98), the Frenchmen were a perfectly suited midfield duo – Petit the holding anchor, Vieira the dynamic, rangy

IT'S A WORLD KNOCKOUT

Europe isn't alone in having a rich history of club football competitions. Fans around the world can cheer on their teams in tournaments that cross continents (see the top line, right) or simply bring together teams from the same country. All in the hope of lifting that coveted trophy.

AFC CHAMPIONS LEAGUE
Founded 1967:
Asian Champion Club Tournament
32 teams (group stage)
Most wins Pohang Steelers (3)
Winners by nation:
11 South Korea
5 Japan
4 Saudi Arabia
3 Iran
3 Israel
3 China

CAF CHAMPIONS LEAGUE
Founded 1964:
African Club Champions Cup
55 teams (2017)
Most wins Al Ahly (8)
Winners by nation:
14 Egypt
6 DR Congo
5 Algeria
5 Morocco
5 Cameroon

USA
MLS CUP
Founded 1996
12 teams
(play-offs)
Most wins
LA Galaxy (5)

BRAZIL
COPA DA BRASIL
Founded 1989
91 teams (2017)
Most wins
Grêmio (5)

ARGENTINA
COPA ARGENTINA
Founded 1969
99 teams
(2016–17)
Most wins
Boca Juniors (3)

CHILE
COPA CHILE
Founded 1958
32 teams
Most wins
Colo-Colo (11)

MEXICO
COPA MX
Founded 1907
27 teams
(2017)
Most wins
(from 1943 –
professional era)
Léon, Club América,
Puebla (5)

CONCACAF CHAMPIONS LEAGUE
Founded 1962: Champions' Cup
24 teams (group stage)
Most wins Club América (7)
Winners by nation:
32 Mexico
6 Costa Rica
3 El Salvador
2 Suriname, Honduras, Trinidad & Tobago, Guatemala, USA, Haiti

COPA LIBERTADORES
Founded 1960
44 teams (2017)
Most wins Independiente (7)
Winners by nation:
24 Argentina
17 Brazil
8 Uruguay
3 Colombia
3 Paraguay

OFC CHAMPIONS LEAGUE
Founded 1987: Oceania Club Championship
16 teams (group stage)
Most wins Auckland City (8)
Winners by nation:
10 New Zealand
4 Australia (now AFC member)
1 Papua New Guinea

EGYPT
EGYPT CUP
Founded 1921
32 teams (main tournament)
Most wins Al Ahly (35)

SOUTH KOREA
KOREAN FA CUP
Founded 1996
83 teams (2016)
Most wins Pohang Steelers, Suwon Samsung Bluewings (4)

JAPAN
EMPEROR'S CUP
Founded 1921
88 teams (2016)
Most wins Keio University (9)

CHINA
CHINESE FA CUP
Founded 1995
64 teams (2016)
Most wins Shandong Luneng Taishan (5)

AUSTRALIA
FFA CUP
Founded 2014
704 teams (2016)
Most wins Adelaide United, Melbourne Victory, Melbourne City (1)

THE WHOLE WORLD CUP

It began in Uruguay in 1930, with 13 teams from Europe, North America and South America. Since then, 19 World Cups have followed, involving nations from all the inhabited continents. Here is the visual story of the 82 World Cup countries – most still with us, some lost to history.

- Entry to World Cup finals
- World Cup champion
- Host nation

NORTH AMERICA — **SOUTH AMERICA** — **EUROPE**

Years (top to bottom): 2014, 2010, 2006, 2002, 1998, 1994, 1990, 1986, 1982, 1978, 1974, 1970, 1966, 1962, 1958, 1954, 1950, 1938, 1934, 1930

Countries (left to right): CANADA, USA, MEXICO, EL SALVADOR, HONDURAS, COSTA RICA, CUBA, JAMAICA, HAITI, TRINIDAD & TOBAGO, ECUADOR, PERU, COLOMBIA, CHILE, ARGENTINA, BOLIVIA, BRAZIL, PARAGUAY, URUGUAY, REPUBLIC OF IRELAND, NORTHERN IRELAND, SCOTLAND, WALES, ENGLAND, PORTUGAL, SPAIN, FRANCE, BELGIUM, NETHERLANDS, NORWAY, SWEDEN, DENMARK, GERMANY, WEST GERMANY, EAST GERMANY, SWITZERLAND, ITALY, AUSTRIA, CZECHOSLOVAKIA, CZECH REPUBLIC, SLOVAKIA

European winners

4 West Germany/Germany
4 Italy
1 England
1 France
1 Spain

South American winners

5 Brazil
2 Uruguay
2 Argentina

AFRICA

ASIA & OCEANIA

2014
2010
2006
2002
1998
1994
1990
1986
1982
1978
1974
1970
1966
1962
1958
1954
1950
1938
1934
1930

POLAND
YUGOSLAVIA
CROATIA
SLOVENIA
BOSNIA & HERZEGOVINA
SERBIA
SERBIA & MONTENEGRO
HUNGARY
GREECE
UKRAINE
ROMANIA
BULGARIA
TURKEY
ISRAEL
SOVIET UNION
RUSSIA
SENEGAL
MOROCCO
IVORY COAST
ALGERIA
TUNISIA
GHANA
TOGO
NIGERIA
CAMEROON
ZAIRE
ANGOLA
SOUTH AFRICA
EGYPT
SAUDI ARABIA
IRAQ
KUWAIT
IRAN
UNITED ARAB EMIRATES
CHINA PR
SOUTH KOREA
NORTH KOREA
JAPAN
DUTCH EAST INDIES
AUSTRALIA
NEW ZEALAND

73

FINAL FORMATIONS

Football tactical fashions come, go and come again. In 20 World Cups,
12 different line-ups have triumphed in the final – just showing that
there's no such thing as the perfect formation. If in doubt, though,
you might want to try 4–2–4, which has fared better than most.

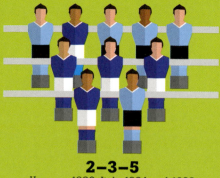

2–3–5
Uruguay 1930, Italy 1934 and 1938

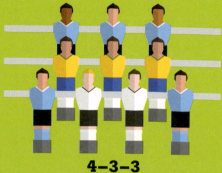

4–3–3
Uruguay 1950, Brazil 1962, Germany 2014

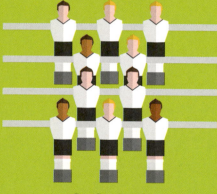

3–2–2–3
West Germany 1954

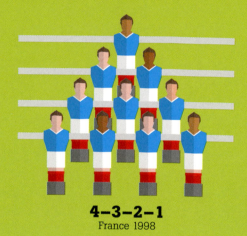

4–3–2–1
France 1998

4–4–2
England 1966, Brazil 1994

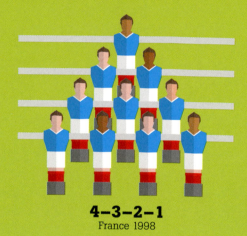

5–2–3
Italy 1982

3–5–2
Argentina 1986

5–3–2
West Germany 1990

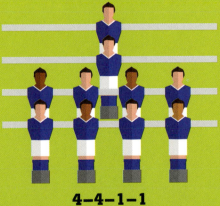

4–4–1–1
Italy 2006

4–2–3–1
Spain 2010

4–2–4
Brazil 1958 and 1970, West Germany 1974,
Argentina 1978

3–4–3
Brazil 2002

PREMIER LEAGUE ... BY THE NUMBERS

The Premier League took over from the old First Division in 1992–93 as England's top professional football league. It's now the richest, most-watched league on the planet, with a TV audience of 3 billion – 40 per cent of the world population – who get to see 20 teams battle it out over 38 games.

103
Highest number of goals scored in a season – Chelsea 2009–10. Manchester City scored 102 in 2013–14

310
The most consecutive games played – Brad Friedel, between August 2004 and October 2012

95
The highest points total in the PL – Chelsea 2004–05

1
Fewest games won in a PL season – Derby County 2007–08. They also notched up the fewest number of points: 11

9–0
Manchester United v Ipswich Town, 1995 – heaviest defeat in PL

65%
The win ratio for Sir Alex Ferguson when manager of Manchester United in PL – played 808, won 527, lost 114

730 MILLION
Number of homes that are reached by the PL

16 YEARS 65 DAYS
Youngest player in PL – Matthew Briggs, Fulham, 2007

260
Number of goals scored by Alan Shearer – the PL record. It took him 434 games

9.7 SECONDS
Fastest goal in PL – Ledley King for Tottenham v Bradford City, December 2000

2 MINUTES, 56 SECONDS
Fastest hat-trick – Sadio Mané for Southampton v Aston Villa, May 2015

632
Appearances in PL by Ryan Giggs – all for Manchester United

0
Number of English managers who have won the Premier League

6
Number of teams that have won the PL:
Manchester United **13**
Chelsea **4**
Arsenal **3**
Manchester City **2**
Blackburn Rovers **1**
Leicester City **1**

BUNDESLIGA ... BY THE NUMBERS

It all began in 1963 with 16 teams, and FC Köln the first champions of the new Bundesliga – which simply means 'Federal League'. Since then, the top German competition has grown to 18 teams and attracts the highest average crowds of any league in the world.

8
Titles won by manager Udo Lattek: Bayern Munich (1971–72, 1972–73, 1973–74, 1984–85, 1985–86, 1986–87), Borussia Mönchengladbach (1975–76, 1976–77)

16 YEARS 335 DAYS
Age of Nuri Şahin – youngest Bundesliga player, Borussia Dortmund, 2005. Also the youngest player to score in the league

832
Matches overseen by manager Otto Rehhagel, including 14 years at Werder Bremen (1981–95)

365
Record number of goals scored by Gerd Müller in the Bundesliga, all for Bayern Munich, 1964–79

12-0
Biggest win, Borussia Mönchengladbach v Borussia Dortmund, 29 April 1978

0
Clubs from the former East Germany or from Berlin that have won the Bundesliga

442
Consecutive games played by Josef 'Sepp' Maier for Bayern Munich between August 1966 and June 1979

204
Number of clean sheets kept by keeper Oliver Kahn in 557 matches, for Karlsruher SC and Bayern Munich, with whom he won 8 Bundesliga titles

43,300
Average attendance at Bundesliga games 2015–16 – the world's highest

602
Record number of appearances for Karl-Heinz Körbel, all for Eintracht Frankfurt 1972–91

25
Bundesliga titles won by Bayern Munich, out of 53. And the rest:
Borussia Dortmund; Borussia Mönchengladbach **5**
Werder Bremen **4**
Hamburger SV; VfB Stuttgart **3**
FC Köln; FC Kaiserslautern **2**
TSV 1860 Munich; Eintracht Braunschweig; FC Nürnberg; VfL Wolfsburg **1**

80,667
Capacity of Borussia Dortmund's Signal Iduna Park stadium – biggest in the Bundesliga

MIDFIELD MAESTROS

Every great football team has had at its centre a player of huge vision, ability and authority to conduct his team-mates as they perform their parts like a well-drilled orchestra. Such a player could not only win the ball, link defence and attack and play a killer pass, but also produce solo moments of memorable brilliance. Bravo to these midfield virtuosos!

XAVI

Played 1998–
Few footballing brains have been as sharp as that of Xavi, an integral part of great days for Spain (one World Cup and two European Championships) and Barcelona (eight La Ligas and four Champions Leagues). No one has passed as accurately or assisted his team-mates as tirelessly.

BOBBY CHARLTON

Played 1956–76
With a dodgy hairstyle but the sweetest of shooting feet, Charlton could glide up and down the pitch all day long, making pinpoint passes and scoring glorious goals for both Manchester United and England. His 49 goals for England included three en route to the 1966 World Cup final.

JOHAN CRUYFF

Played 1964–84
One of the few players to have a move – the 'Cruyff turn' – named after him, the Dutchman brought supreme elegance and skill to Ajax, Barcelona and the Netherlands. He also helped to invent the revolutionary 'total football' style.

MICHEL PLATINI

Played 1972–87
The only player to win the Ballon d'Or three years running (1983–85), Platini was the beating heart of a great French team – winners of the European Championship in 1984. He combined amazing vision and brilliant passing from either foot with a keen eye for goal.

DIEGO MARADONA

Played 1976–97
Only 1.65m (5ft 5in) tall, but strong as an ox and blessed with dribbling skills from heaven, the supremely gifted little Argentinian was also an inspirational captain, leading his country to World Cup victory in 1986.

ZICO

Played 1971–94
One of the best players never to win a World Cup, Zico brought sublime passing, tactical flair and lethal scoring to a brilliant Brazilian team. In 71 games he netted 48 times.

MICHAEL LAUDRUP

Played 1981–98
You don't run the midfield at four legendary clubs (Juventus, Barcelona, Real Madrid and Ajax), winning seven league titles, without a touch of genius. Laudrup was the most graceful of players, famed for his dribbling, where he would switch the ball from one foot to the other before any defender could blink.

FRANK RIJKAARD

Played 1980–95
One of the finest defensive midfielders, Rijkaard helped the Netherlands to its one major footballing triumph, the 1988 European Championship. The Dutchman was almost the complete player – a rock in defence, classy on the ball, equally confident with head and feet, and possessing a thunderous shot.

ZINEDINE ZIDANE

Played 1989–2006: Cannes, Bordeaux, Juventus, Real Madrid, France
Three-time holder of the FIFA World Player of the Year, Zidane had an equally gifted left and right foot, and was just as strong in the air, as he showed by powering home two headers against Brazil in the World Cup final of 1998. He was not the fastest of midfielders, but his vision, close control and balance were razor-sharp.

PELÉ

Played 1956–77
Was he really an attacker or a midfielder? Well, Pelé was equally adept in both roles, with an amazing strike rate of 77 goals in 91 games for Brazil. No other footballer has matched his strength, balance, control, dribbling ability or scoring prowess. Nor has anyone equalled his three World Cup wins (1958, 1962, 1970).

WHO ARE YOU CALLING 'PSYCHO'?!

Often, the name a footballer was born with just isn't enough, so football fans or the media come up with something heroic, derogatory or just plain silly. And, unfairly or otherwise, those nicknames stick like glue. Take a tour around these imaginative designations.

The Fifth Beatle
GEORGE BEST

Good looks, great style and a 1960s heyday shared with the Fab Four – inevitable that the Northern Irish footballing genius should be a shoo-in as an imaginary extra Beatle.

Dave
GUYLAIN NDUMBU-NSUNGU

Bit of a mouthful for supporters, that name – much easier to shout out a single syllable to identify the Congolese forward.

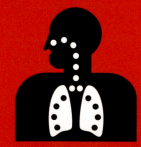

Three Lungs
JI-SUNG PARK

To his Manchester United teammates, it seemed as if the tireless midfielder must have one more lung than the rest.

Wireless
PHILIPP LAHM

Also known as 'The Magic Dwarf', German captain Lahm received the technological nickname for his ability to play anywhere on the pitch.

The Galloping Major
FERENC PUSKÁS

The great forward could certainly gallop his way through a helpless defence, while 'major' referred to his pre-Real Madrid days, playing for the Hungarian army team Budapest Honvéd.

The Butcher of Bilbao
ANDONI GOIKOETXEA

One to avoid in the tackle – just ask Maradona, who had his ankle ligaments shredded by the Athletic Bilbao defender in 1983.

Calamity James
DAVID JAMES

A neat reworking of Calamity Jane (the 19th-century American frontierswoman) and earned for some high-profile goalkeeping gaffes – alongside, it should be said, 169 clean sheets in 572 Premier League games.

Gronaldo
JEAN-CLAUDE DARCHEVILLE

A passion for fast food set the French Guianan striker up for a comparison with the sometimes hefty Brazilian star Ronaldo.

The Flea
LIONEL MESSI

He's small, buzzes everywhere and drives defenders mad – simple, but apt.

Psycho
STUART PEARCE

Facing the ever-determined England left back could be a scary prospect for an opponent – be afraid, be very afraid.

The Wardrobe
PAPA BOUBA DIOP

The former Senegalese midfielder was as big as – yes, you've guessed it – a wardrobe.

The Blind Venetian
MASSIMO TAIBI

Harsh, perhaps, but one of the cleverest of nicknames was well earned by the Italian goalkeeper during a hapless spell at Manchester United.

Duncan Disorderly
DUNCAN FERGUSON

A genius nickname – courtesy of four assault convictions notched up by the big Scottish striker.

The Non-flying Dutchman
DENNIS BERGKAMP

Skills beyond compare – but the airborne phobia of the man from the Netherlands was just too tempting for football fan wit.

Wizard of Oz
HARRY KEWELL

A winger from Australia with tricks up his sleeve – what else could you call him?

Sicknote
DARREN ANDERTON

An injury-plagued career, including no fewer than five hernia operations, won the England midfielder one of the cruelest of nicknames.

Kun
SERGIO AGÜERO

It says 'Kun Agüero' on the Argentine star's shirt – thanks to his brothers, who thought little Sergio looked just like the Japanese anime cave-boy character Kum Kum.

Hulk
GIVANILDO VIEIRA DE SOUZA

Yes, he's big, but it's the Brazilian striker's likeness to Lou Ferrigno – the actor who played the Hulk in the original TV series of *The Incredible Hulk* – that won him the name.

The Kaiser
FRANZ BECKENBAUER

Captain of West Germany, a World Cup legend, a man to respect who oozes style – just like an emperor, really.

The Divine Ponytail
ROBERTO BAGGIO

Yes, the Italian striker wore a ponytail, and his footballing skills – and devout Buddhist faith – were out of this world.

Snowflake
RONALD KOEMAN

Doesn't sound appropriate for the burly Dutch defender, now manager – but the name hails from his days as a Barcelona player, when his ultra-fair hair was compared to a celebrity albino gorilla – called Snowflake – at the local zoo.

The Baby-faced Assassin
OLE GUNNAR SOLSKJAER

Ah, such cute boyish looks, but the Norwegian goal-poacher could kill off many a team with his deadly striking.

Ibracadabra
ZLATAN IBRAHIMOVIĆ

The Swedish striker is a magician with the ball at his feet, and magicians say 'abracadabra!' – see what the fans did there?

THE SACK RACE

Well paid? Yes. Stressful? Certainly. It's a tough job managing a football team, and such are the demands at big clubs that most managers will barely have a season to get it right, while a special few ride the storms and enter football folklore. Witness these quickie football divorces and long and happy marriages.

QUICK EXITS

2004
Luigi Delneri
0 GAMES, 36 DAYS
FC Porto
José Mourinho's replacement at Porto, who had previously lifted Italian Serie B side Chievo Verona into Serie A, was sacked before the season began – allegedly for bad timekeeping. Delneri was also sacked in 1998 as manager of Empoli before the season had started.

1975
Brian Clough
8 GAMES, 44 DAYS
Leeds United
Clough was flying high after winning the English First Division title with Derby County but fell out with Leeds' star players, such as Johnny Giles and Billy Bremner. He lost three of his six league games in charge. The sack and a big payoff followed.

2009
Jörg Berger
1 GAME, 5 DAYS
Arminia Bielefeld
Berger, a former manger of Eintracht Frankfurt and Schalke 04, was brought in for the final game of the 2008–09 Bundesliga season to help the club avoid relegation. Arminia Bielefeld drew 2-2 with Hannover 96, finished bottom and Berger exited.

2011
Serse Cosmi
4 GAMES, 34 DAYS
Palermo
Despite a victory over AC Milan, Cosmi oversaw three defeats with Serie A club Palermo, including an unforgivable 4-0 drubbing by fellow Sicilians Calcio Catania.

2007
Leroy Rosenior
0 GAMES, 10 MINUTES
Torquay United
Newly relegated from England's League Two, Torquay turned to Rosenior, the man who had led the club from 2002 to 2006. A matter of moments after the announcement, just as the club changed ownership, he was sacked.

1978
Jock Stein
10 GAMES, 44 DAYS
Leeds United
Uncannily, Stein lasted exactly the same length of time as Clough, but the former Celtic manager left under less of a cloud to become manager of Scotland. He won four of his ten games in charge at Leeds.

LONG HAUL

20
(20 YEARS AND COUNTING)
Arsène Wenger
ARSENAL
1996–
Wenger was a relative unknown when he moved from the Japanese team Nagoya Grampus Eight in 1996. Now he is Arsenal's longest-serving and most successful manager, leading the team to three Premier League titles and six FA Cups.

44
(44 YEARS – WORLD RECORD)
Guy Roux
AUXERRE
1961–2005
In 1961, Auxerre were an obscure third-tier side, but Roux, who also played for the club (1952–61), made them Ligue 1 champions and four-time winners of the Coupe de France. Along the way, he coached Eric Cantona, Laurent Blanc and Basile Boli.

25
(25 YEARS)
Matt Busby
MANCHESTER UNITED
1945–69, 1970–71
Given the last rites after the Munich air disaster in 1958 that killed seven of his players, Busby went on to lead United to European Cup glory in 1968 to add to five league titles. Fellow Scot Alex Ferguson overtook Busby's reign by two years (1986–2013).

29
(29 YEARS)
Ronnie McFall
PORTADOWN
1986–2016
McFall took Portadown to four Northern Ireland Premiership titles and three Irish Cups. Previously, he coached Glentoran, where he had played for four years.

14
(14 YEARS)
Thomas Schaaf
WERDER BREMEN
1999–2013
A true one-club man, Schaaf played for 17 years for Bremen (1978–95) before managing the reserve team and then the first. He took the club to its first double – Bundesliga and DFB-Pokal – in 2003–04.

NATIONAL TREASURES

GIAMPAOLO MAZZA
SAN MARINO
1998–2013 (15 years)
✸ oversaw one victory and three draws in 83 games – win percentage 1.2%

HELMUT SCHÖN
WEST GERMANY
1964–78 (14 years)
✸ coached the most World Cup matches – 25
✸ most World Cup wins – 16

WALTER WINTERBOTTOM
ENGLAND
1946–62 (16 years)
✸ won 78 and drew 33 of his 139 games – win percentage 56.1%

MESSI MAGIC v RONALDO SWAGGER

The Barcelona and Real Madrid stars are arguably the best footballers on the planet, playing for arguably the greatest clubs. Since Ronaldo joined Messi in La Liga in 2009, the two have been constantly compared. But who is better? Look at these stats, covering five years from the 2009–10 season up to December 2014, and you'll see there's not much in it.

TOTAL
259
GOALS

239
APPS

219 GOALS SCORED INSIDE THE BOX

40 GOALS SCORED OUTSIDE THE BOX

32 PENALTIES SCORED

13 FREE KICKS SCORED

AMAZING FACT!
Barcelona snapped up 13-year-old prodigy Lionel in December 2000. The contract was signed on a restaurant napkin – the closest piece of paper to hand. That napkin could turn out to be one of the most valuable documents in football history.

10
HEADED GOALS

BARCELONA

10.4%

73.8%   **15.8%**

WITH MESSI STARTING

- **WIN RATE**
- **DRAW RATE**
- **LOSS RATE**

42
RIGHT-FOOTED GOALS

207
LEFT-FOOTED GOALS

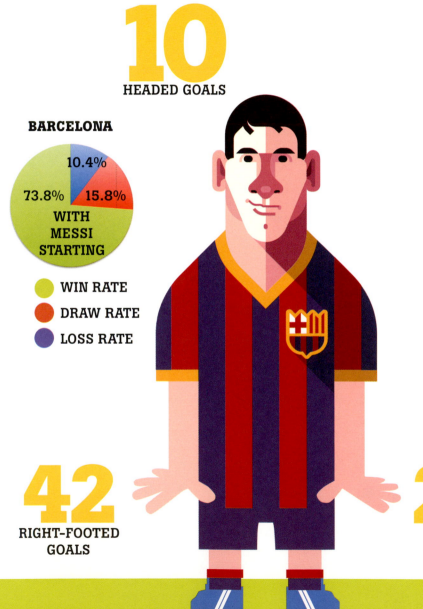

TOTAL
256
GOALS
234
APPS

214 GOALS SCORED INSIDE THE BOX

42 GOALS SCORED OUTSIDE THE BOX

49 PENALTIES SCORED

23 FREE KICKS SCORED

AMAZING FACT!
Ronaldo's free-kick speed is around 130 km/h (80 mph). His incredible heading prowess is helped by an ability to jump 44cm (17in) from a standing start, generating 5g of G-force, five times the power of a cheetah in full flight.

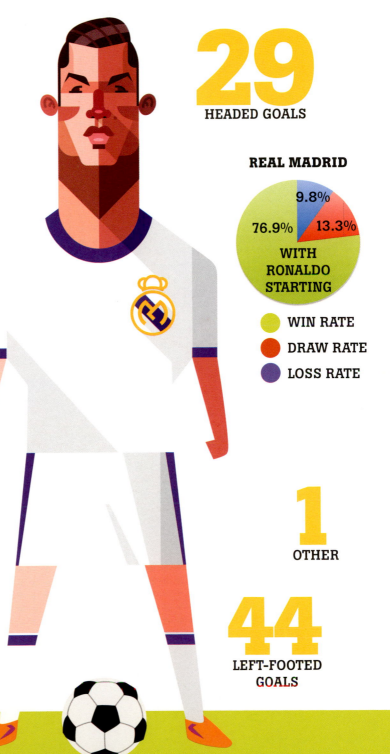

29
HEADED GOALS

REAL MADRID

9.8%

76.9%   13.3%

WITH RONALDO STARTING

⬤ WIN RATE
⬤ DRAW RATE
⬤ LOSS RATE

1
OTHER

182
RIGHT-FOOTED GOALS

44
LEFT-FOOTED GOALS

TOTAL DISAPPOINTMENTS

Puskás and Hungary, 1954, Cruyff and the Netherlands, 1974 – captains each, two of the best players of all time and two of the greatest teams. Everyone's favourites to win the World Cup, and yet they both lost the final, out-thought on each occasion by the super-efficient Germans.

MANAGER:
GUSTÁV SEBES

1
GYULA GROSICS

2
JENÖ BUZÁNSZKY

3
GYULA LÓRÁNT

4
MIHÁLY LANTOS

5
JÓZSEF BOZSIK

6
JÓZSEF ZAKARIÁS

11
ZOLTÁN CZIBOR

9
NÁNDOR HIDEGKUTI

20
MIHÁLY TÓTH

8
SÁNDOR KOCSIS

10
FERENC PUSKÁS (c)

HUNGARY, WORLD CUP FINAL, 4 JULY 1954, WANKDORF STADIUM, BERN

The 'Golden Team' were on a four-year, 36-game unbeaten run, during which they had won the 1952 Olympic football gold and dealt out 6–3 and 7–1 humiliations to England. Come the final, though, the Hungarians were still recovering from a gruelling 120-minute semifinal against the almost-as-amazing Uruguayans. The West Germans took skilful advantage of this, a leaky defence, rainy conditions and a less-than-fit Puskás to win 3–2.

MANAGER:
RINUS MICHELS

8
JAN JONGBLOED

20 **WIM SUURBIER**

17 **WIM RIJSBERGEN**

2 **ARIE HAAN**

12 **RUUD KROL**

6 **WIM JANSEN**

13 **JOHAN NEESKENS**

3 **WILLEM VAN HANEGEM**

16 **JOHNNY REP**

14 **JOHAN CRUYFF (c)**

15 **ROB RENSENBRINK**

NETHERLANDS, WORLD CUP FINAL, 7 JULY 1974, OLYMPIC STADIUM, MUNICH

Manager of the Netherlands team for barely four months, Rinus Michels had already instilled in them his concept of 'total football', honed while coaching Ajax and Barcelona, aided and abetted by the brilliant feet and footballing brain of captain Johan Cruyff. The sublime fluidity of the Dutch had dazzled spectators, but the men in orange came up against a vastly talented West German side, already 1972 European Champions, who triumphed 2–1.

ARE YOU BLIND, REF?!

Who would be a referee? You get 90 minutes of verbal abuse from players and spectators, every split-second decision is recorded and analyzed, with the good ones forgotten, while you're bashed over the head for the bad ones. It's a thankless task – so pity the refs who made these big-time blunders.

Goalie GBH

CHARLES CORVER
Netherlands
West Germany 3–3 France
(5–4 on penalties)
World Cup semifinal 1982

• Ten minutes into the second half, France midfielder Michel Platini plays a perfect through ball to Patrick Battiston, who is then clattered by the full force of West German goalkeeper Harald Schumacher. It's a horrible collision that leaves Battiston unconscious, with broken teeth and damaged vertebrae. The ref takes no action against Schumacher, not even a yellow card, with the keeper going on to save the shoot-out penalty that took the Germans to the final.

The phantom goal

HANS-JOACHIM OSMERS Germany
Bayern Munich 2–1 FC Nürnberg
Bundesliga 1994

• It's the end of the season and Nürnberg are fighting for their Bundesliga lives. At 0–0, Bayern take a corner and Bayern defender Thomas Helmer scrambles the ball wide of the far post. Astonishingly, the linesman thinks the ball has gone in and so the referee awards the goal. Nürnberg then miss a penalty and Bayern go on to win 2–1. The match was replayed after an appeal, but Bayern won 5–0 and Nürnberg were relegated.

Three for the price of two

GRAHAM POLL England
Croatia 2–2 Australia
World Cup group match 2006

• Croatian left back Josip Šimunić gets one yellow card and then commits another bookable offence. Out comes the yellow card again but he isn't sent off. Poll did finally get round to showing Šimunić the red after dishing out a third yellow card for dissent.

Sweet revenge

JORGE LARRIONDA Uruguay
England 1–4 Germany
World Cup second round 2010

• It's 2–1. England have just pulled a goal back and Frank Lampard shoots, the ball hits the crossbar and then clearly crosses the goal line – except, if you're the ref, it doesn't. For all Germans, it's payback time for Geoff Hurst's debatable third goal against them in the 1966 World Cup final.

Waving for the Mexicans

ALI HUSSEIN KANDIL Egypt
Mexico 4–0 El Salvador
World Cup group match 1970

• Just before half-time, El Salvador, in their first World Cup, think they have won a free kick – or is it a throw-in? In the confusion, Mexico take a quick free kick, the referee allows play to go on and Mexico score. The El Salvador players then refuse to take the kick-off and Kandil blows early for half-time.

Kung-fu fighting

HOWARD WEBB England
Spain 1–0 Netherlands
World Cup final 2010

• It was the dirtiest end to a World Cup, with Webb brandishing 14 yellow cards – the most in a final. But when Nigel de Jong decided to kung-fu kick Spanish defender Xabi Alonso squarely in the chest, then one yellow should really have been a red. It took until the 110th minute before Webb did get round to sending a player off, Dutchman John Heitinga.

A case of mistaken identity

ANDRE MARRINER England
Chelsea 6–0 Arsenal
Premier League 2014

• Eden Hazard of Chelsea shoots at goal and the ball is saved acrobatically – not by the goalkeeper but by Arsenal's Alex Oxlade-Chamberlain. It's clearly a penalty and a red card, but what's this? Marriner has sent off Kieran Gibbs and not Oxlade-Chamberlain. A true case of 'Get your eyes tested, ref!'

Only the ref will ever know …

KOMAN COULIBALY Mali
USA 2–2 Slovenia
World Cup group match 2010

• Moving into the final 5 minutes, the USA swing a free kick into the penalty area. After much pushing and shoving, Maurice Edu bursts through and scores.

The referee has blown, though, and the goal doesn't stand. Was Edu offside? No. Didn't the ref see the USA players being held in the box? Apparently so. Coulibaly, who was not to referee again in the World Cup, has never given a reason.

Not seeing red

KARL-JOSEF ASSENMACHER
Germany
Netherlands 2–0 England
World Cup qualifier 1993

• With the game tied at 0–0, England midfielder David Platt bears down on the Dutch goal with only the keeper to beat. He is then hauled down right on the edge of the penalty area by Ronald Koeman. Assenmacher awards a free kick rather than a penalty – but what truly amazes is a yellow card for Koeman and not a straight red. To add insult to injury, Koeman then scores a peach of a free kick to make it 1–0. FIFA relieved Assenmacher of his duties for his next match and he never refereed an international again.

Are you blind drunk, ref?!

SERGEI SHMOLIK Belarus
FC Vitebsk 1–1 FC Naftan
Belarus Premier League 2008

Something was not quite right with 43-year-old Sergei Shmolik, voted best Belarusian referee in 2007. He had barely left the centre circle, refused to hand out any cards and was gesticulating in a strange way. Eventually, Shmolik was escorted, reluctantly, from the pitch, while waving to the crowd. He claimed he had a 'bad back' but was found to have high levels of alcohol in his blood, courtesy of a pre-match vodka binge. A suspension soon followed.

FALLING FOR IT

Sometimes footballers just can't resist taking a tumble – to win a free kick or penalty, or even get another player into trouble. There are those, though, who have raised this to an art form, incorporating mime, acrobatics, acting genius and pure slapstick. Sit back and admire this stellar XI.

Perfect 10 for the perfect dive

JÜRGEN KLINSMANN Germany
West Germany v Argentina
1990 Word Cup final, Rome
• Klinsmann cuts inside from the right wing and is 'challenged' by the Argentine defender Pedro Monzón. The German launches into space, falls to ground and performs a balletic 'Dying Swan' routine. Klinsmann later protested, 'If he didn't make contact with me, how come I had a 15cm gash in my shin?'
RESULT *Red card for Monzón, World Cup for West Germany*

Slapstick stumble

PAUL ALCOCK England, referee
Sheffield Wednesday v Arsenal
Premier League, 1998
• Paulo Di Canio comes to blows with Arsenal's Martin Keown and gets the red card from referee Paul Alcock. Di Canio takes exception and pushes the ref in the chest. Alcock then staggers backwards for some distance and falls over in a move that would have made Buster Keaton proud.
RESULT *Di Canio is banned for 11 matches and fined £10,000*

Give the man an Oscar

CRISTIANO RONALDO Portugal
Real Madrid v AC Milan
Champions League, 2010
• A small touchline scuffle results in Milan's Ignazio Abate lightly brushing the face of Ronaldo. The Portuguese then produces an award-winning performance as he clutches his face, falls, writhes around, looks up to assess the situation, then rolls some more. Milan hardman Gennaro Gattuso stands over Ronaldo as if intent on finishing off the job.
RESULT *Much commotion but no card for Abate*

NEYMAR
Brazil

Fall guy?

Neymar da Silva Santos Júnior is a prodigiously talented striker for both Barcelona and Brazil, but he has gained a reputation for going to ground too easily. As Fabio Capello said in 2014, 'Neymar is a great striker, but I hate that a player of his level has to fall to the ground every time you touch him.' However, the captaincy of his country, bestowed in 2014, helped to make Neymar a more 'upright' person.

Corner-kick capers

RIVALDO Brazil
Brazil v Turkey
2002 World Cup group match, Ulsan, S. Korea
• Rivaldo is about to take a corner. Turkish player Hakan Ünsal kicks the ball at him, stikes his leg and the Brazilian collapses, clutching his face.
RESULT *Ünsal is sent off, but Rivaldo is later fined more than £5,000 for feigning injury*

Getting the kick-back

DIEGO SIMEONE Argentina
Argentina v England
1998 World Cup quarterfinal
• England's David Beckham, floored by a push in the back from Simeone, then gives the Argentine defender a quick kick to the back of the thigh. Not clever, and right in front of the referee, but Simeone goes down easily and joins in the pleas for Beckham's dismissal.
RESULT *Red card – and months of abuse – for Beckham, yellow card and bogeyman status for Simeone*

Deceptive handiwork

BRYAN CARRASCO Chile
Chile v Ecuador, 2011, under-20s international
• Tightly marking Edson Montaño, Carrasco grabs the Ecuadorian's arm from behind and uses it to smack himself in the face. He then falls to the ground as if polelaxed.
RESULT *A free kick – one of the least justified ever – to Chile*

Falling over himself

ARTURO VIDAL Chile
Juventus v Real Madrid
Champions League, 2013
• Vidal bursts into the Real penalty box, shapes to shoot, misses the ball, kicks a chunk out of the pitch and takes a spectacular fall. He then has the cheek to chase after the ref, claiming a penalty.
RESULT *An insult to the ref's intelligence, and eyesight – no penalty*

Sneaky peek

DIDIER DROGBA Ivory Coast
Chelsea v Napoli
Champions League, 2012
• Napoli's Salvatore Aronica is on the attack. Drogba tracks the man closely and then lurches backwards in dramatic fashion, clutching his face as if elbowed by the Italian. Replays suggest no contact. As he lies, prostrate, on the turf, Drogba is caught on camera opening a crafty eye to check on proceedings.
RESULT *No card for Aronica, but he's soon substituted and Chelsea win to reach the quarterfinal*

Going head-to-head

NORBERT MEIER Germany, manager
ALBERT STREIT Germany
MSV Duisburg v FC Köln
Bundesliga, 2005
• Streit bundles a Duisburg player off the pitch, and Meier, the Duisburg manager, squares up to him on the touchline. Their heads meet and Meier pitches backwards as if dealt a powerful blow. Streit hits the ground, too. Mayhem ensues, though on closer inspection it was clearly Meier who administered the, albeit feeble, head-butt.
RESULT *Streit is sent off, while Meier, his playacting caught on camera, is sacked by his club and banned from management for three months*

Bluffing masterclass

ARJEN ROBBEN Netherlands
Netherlands v Mexico
2014 World Cup, round of 16
• Robben has history on the diving front and he saved probably his best effort for the dying seconds of this crucial World Cup tie, throwing himself acrobatically into the air after the faintest of touches from Mexican captain Rafael Márquez. Robben had already tried to win a penalty earlier in the game – an effort he later admitted was a dive.
RESULT *Yellow card for Márquez, goal and a World Cup quarterfinal for the Netherlands*

PUTTING THE BOOT IN

A footballer's most important piece of equipment, the boot still does the same job it always has – providing grip, protecting the feet against the elements and giving impetus to the ball. But boots have evolved with new technologies and the demands for ever–greater performance.

1900s to 1940s

Up to the end of the Second World War, boots kept to the same high-sided, thick-leather, long-laced formula. A number of still-familiar boot makers emerged in these years, including Gola in England (1905) and Hummel in Germany (1923). After the war, a South American style of lighter, more flexible boot began to catch on.

1890s

In 1891, a revision of the laws allowed football boots to have both studs and bars, so long as they were made of leather. Players would have several pairs of boots with studs of different length, depending on ground conditions.

1950s to 1960s
ADIDAS ARGENTINA
HELMUT RAHN

Adidas boots, with screw-in studs, gave West Germany, including striker Helmut Rahn, an advantage over Hungary in a 1954 World Cup final played in rain-soaked, slippery condtions. Rahn scored two in the 3–2 victory.

ADIDAS

The oh-so-familiar company gets its name from the founder, Adolf ('Adi') Dassler. He and his brother Rudolf ('Rudi') began making sports shoes in 1924 in their mother's Bavarian laundry, under the name Gebrüder Dassler Schuhfabrik (Dassler Brothers Shoe Factory). After the Second World War, the brothers went their separate ways, Adi to form Adidas, Rudi to create Puma and, in 1952, the first boot with screw-in studs.

The three Adidas stripes made their first appearance in 1949, soon after Adi had founded the company, which then won fame in 1954 with the surprise victory in the World Cup of a West German team clad in Adidas boots. Suddenly, everyone wanted 'the boots that won the World Cup', which were half the weight but twice the price of their English equivalents. Today, Adidas vies with Nike for the lion's share of world boot sales.

Mid 1960s
ADIDAS DIAMANT
GEOFF HURST, BOBBY MOORE

At the 1966 World Cup, 75 per cent of players wore Adidas boots, including Bobby Moore and Geoff Hurst, who scored his three goals in the final wearing the Diamant.

1970
STYLO MATCHMAKER
GEORGE BEST

Best's autograph was printed in gold on the side of the Matchmaker, made from soft leather for lightness, flexibility and comfort. The boot was also distinguished by its white polyurethane sole and short, asymmetric laces.

1970s to 1980s
PUMA KING
PELÉ, JOHAN CRUYFF, DIEGO MARADONA

The German company Puma made the 'Kings' worn by Pelé when he led Brazil to World Cup victory in 1970 and by Maradona when he dribbled past six players to score 'the goal of the century' against England in 1986.

1990s
ADIDAS PREDATOR
DAVID BECKHAM, ZINEDINE ZIDANE

Released in 1994, the Predator was based on an idea from former Liverpool player Craig Johnston, where dimpled rubber patches were applied to the boot for greater control of the ball. Beckham and Zidane were early adopters.

2000s
NIKE MERCURIAL
RONALDO

Nike, the US sportswear company – the world's largest – finally entered the game in 1998 with the Mercurial. Ronaldo, the Brazilian striker, wore Mercurials when he scored eight goals at the 2002 World Cup, including both final goals.

2010s
ADIDAS ADIZERO F50
LIONEL MESSI

The 'zero' was a reference to the lightness of the boot, which at 165g (5.8oz) was the lightest on the market when launched in time for the World Cup in 2010. The micofibre uppers reduced weight while maintaining boot stability.

The future?
ADIDAS SAMBA PRIMEKNIT
LUIS SUÁREZ

In 2014, Adidas released the world's first knitted football boot, given its debut outing by Luis Suárez in a game for Liverpool against Manchester United. The knitted upper makes the boot light and flexible, but also strong.

BACK OF THE (WRONG) NET

Whoops! There's nothing more mortifying than the sight of the ball flying into your own net – off your own boot, head or other unsuspecting part of your anatomy. But it's a million times worse when most of the global population are watching. The World Cup has seen 41 own goals – 1.7 per cent of all tournament goals. Here are the key egg-on-face moments.

1st
WORLD CUP OWN GOAL
MANUEL ROSAS
Mexico
CHILE 3–0 MEXICO
Uruguay 1930

6
MOST OWN GOALS IN A TOURNAMENT
FRANCE 1998
All in group matches

ONLY
PLAYER TO SCORE A GOAL FOR HIS OWN TEAM AND HIS OPPONENTS
ERNIE BRANDTS
Netherlands
NETHERLANDS 2–1 ITALY
Argentina 1978

OLDEST
PLAYER TO SCORE AN OWN GOAL
NOEL VALLADARES
Honduras
37 years 43 days
FRANCE 3–0 HONDURAS
Brazil 2014
• The first World Cup goal to be decided by goal-line technology

2:10
minutes   seconds
FASTEST OWN GOAL
SEAD KOLAŠINAC
Bosnia and Herzegovina
ARGENTINA 2–1 BOSNIA
Brazil 2014

ONLY
OWN GOAL TO BE THE ONLY GOAL OF THE MATCH
CARLOS GAMARRA
Paraguay
ENGLAND 1–0 PARAGUAY
Germany 2006

94 minutes

ONLY OWN GOAL SCORED IN EXTRA TIME

JIMMY DICKINSON

England

ENGLAND 4–4 BELGIUM

Switzerland 1954

ONLY

COUNTRY TO HAVE SCORED MORE GOALS IN THEIR OWN NET THAN IN THEIR OPPONENTS'

TRINIDAD AND TOBAGO

Germany 2006

• 1 own goal in 2–0 defeat by Paraguay, 0 regular goals in all three group games

3 TEAMS

WITH MOST OWN GOALS (3) SCORED

BULGARIA, MEXICO, SPAIN

Bulgaria is the only country to have scored two own goals in the same tournament

England 1966

FIRST

OWN GOAL TO BE SCORED IN AN OPENING MATCH

TOM BOYD

Scotland

BRAZIL 2–1 SCOTLAND

France 1998

ONLY

OWN GOAL TO BE THE FIRST GOAL SCORED IN A WORLD CUP

MARCELO

Brazil

BRAZIL 3–1 CROATIA

11 minutes

Brazil 2014

TAKE YOUR PLACES

Football may be a simple game, but over the past 150 years a lot of thought has gone into getting the ball into the opposing net and stopping it from getting into the home goal. From the earliest days in England, Hungarians, Italians, Brazilians, Dutchmen and others have tinkered with formations to try to create the perfect fusion of defence and attack.

3-2-1-4

1870s

Early football was about all-out attack. England are supposed to have used this formation against Scotland in 1872, with the Scots adopting the 'more cautious' 2–2–6. Amazingly, the game ended 0–0.

1-2-7

early 1950s

Also set out as 3-2-3-2, this was the formation that brought the great Hungarian teams of the 1950s such success. In effect, it included five forwards but with one lying deep to draw out the opposing centre back and create space for the other four. Those strikers would also switch positions, causing further defensive confusion. This development, coupled with lethal finishing from Ferenc Puskás and Sándor Kocsis, led to the 6–3 and 7–1 defeats of England in 1953 and 1954, and the 8–3 thrashing of West Germany in a 1954 World Cup group match.

2-3-5

2-3-2-3

1880s/1890s

As the game became more professional, so formations gained a little more sophistication. Preston North End, winners in 1888–89 of the first English league and the FA Cup, used the 2-3-5 'pyramid' formation, which added some defensive steel and allowed for more passing in the game, a style pioneered by Scottish players.

3-2-2-3

1930s

The Italian national team, under the manager Vittorio Pozzo, made its own, more defensive, changes to the old 2-3-5 formation, producing Il Metodo, or 'The Method', with two forwards pulled back from the front line. This proved to be a highly effective counterattacking style and won Italy two World Cups, in 1934 and 1938.

1920s

Herbert Chapman, Arsenal manager 1925–34, pulled two forwards and one midfielder further down the pitch to create the 'W-M' formation. Using this, Arsenal won five English league titles between 1930 and 1938.

4-2-4

late 1950s

A formation, developed by the Brazilians, that paved the way for most modern line-ups. Though focused on defence, with the first four-man backline, it allowed plenty of width and the flexibility for players to push up or drop back. The formation helped Brazil to World Cup victory in 1958 – and later in 1970.

1960s

The familiar formation that came to dominate European club football in the 1980s and 1990s (favoured by Arrigo Sacchi at AC Milan and Alex Ferguson at Manchester United) found its first significant champion in Alf Ramsay, who took England to victory in the 1966 World Cup. If a little predictable, it offered solid defence, width, ease of possession and support going forward.

4-4-2

1970s

Manager of the Dutch team at the 1974 World Cup, Rinus Michels tore up the formation rule book by introducing 'total football', where players were given licence to roam in and out of position to support or make plays. It needed a genius on the pitch to pull the strings and Michels had that in the great Johan Cruyff. Only the hugely gifted Barcelona team of recent years has come close to emulating this free-flowing style.

?-?-?

2000s

Since the 1980s, many formations have been tried, most of them subtle variations on existing themes. Spain, though, managed by Vicente del Bosque, surprised the world in the 2012 European Championship by fielding a team with six midfielders and no recognized striker, albeit with Cesc Fàbregas playing as a deep-lying forward or 'false number 9'. In fact, the formation had already been tried with some success by Luciano Spalletti, manager of AS Roma, in 2006–07, followed even more successfully by Pep Guardiola's Barcelona team a few years later. It does help if you can field Messi as your 'false number 9'.

4-6-0

TRICKS AND TREATS

Yes, you too can have the skills of Ronaldo, Messi or Neymar. Actually, it takes years of practice and a degree of innate genius, but here's a quick tour around the football tricks that separate the stars from the plodders.

Stepover

Perfected by dribblers such as Robinho and Cristiano Ronaldo, the stepover is a great way to bamboozle a defender. At speed, lift your leading foot, 'step over' the ball, then take it in the oppsite direction with the outside of the other foot.

Overhead kick

Known also as the scissor-kick, the bicycle kick or, in South America, La Chilena ('The Chilean'), the spectacular scoring shot, popularized by Pelé, has some notable modern exponents, including Wayne Rooney and Zlatan Ibrahimović. It requires supreme balance, courage, timing and awareness of where the goal is.

Keepy-uppy

Perhaps the best-known show-off football skill of all, keepy-uppy is actually of limited use in a fast-moving game. The idea is simply to keep the ball in the air, using any part of the body, except the hands, to prevent it hitting the ground. Some amazing records have been set.

Keepy-uppy world record

The English 'professional freestyler' Dan Magness holds the men's world record for endurance keep-uppy. In Hong Kong, in June 2010, he kept a ball in the air, using just his feet, legs and head, for 26 hours. Dan also managed to walk 58km (36 miles) across London in January 2010, keeping a ball up the whole way. In the process of the walk-come-juggle, he visited the stadiums of all five London clubs that were in the Premier League at the time.

Fastest 100m sprint with ball on forehead

An unlikely record, perhaps, but one held by another English football freestyler, Daniel Cutting. He ran the distance in 18.53 seconds without the ball leaving his head. When Daniel married in 2013, he displayed his keepy-uppy skills as he walked down the aisle of the church and then as he waited for his bride to arrive.

Rainbow kick

An outrageous move, but good if you're caught in a tight spot. Using the back foot, roll the ball up the front leg, then flick the ball with the front leg over your head and that of the bemused defender. The skill, brought to wide attention by the Nigerian star Jay-Jay Okocha, has become a Neymar speciality.

The Cruyff turn

1 Shape your body as if you were about to pass or cross the ball.

2 Drag the ball behind your standing leg with the inside of your other foot.

3 Twist your shoulders and hips to get back in line with the ball and then speed off, leaving your marker for dead.

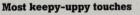

Most keepy-uppy touches

Milene Domingues, first wife of Brazil stiker Ronaldo and winner of 20 caps for the Brazilian women's football team, holds the record for the highest number of touches. In 9 hours and 6 minutes, she managed an incredible 55,187 touches without the ball touching the ground.

Tricky Scot

Not a record but an instance of keepy-uppy used to great effect during a match. On 11 April 1967 – a famous day for Scottish football – with Scotland leading world champions England 3–2 at Wembley, left half Jim Baxter tormented the likes of Bobby Moore and Jack Charlton with some virtuoso displays of the ball-juggling art.

Rabona

In Spanish, *rabona* means 'to play truant'. The cheeky skill, where you wrap your kicking leg behind the other to cross or shoot in an unexpected direction, is said to have been invented by Argentinian Ricardo Infante in a game between Estudiantes and Rosario in 1948.

ULTIMATE DREAM TEAM SHEET?

The 11 best players ever? You could argue over that until the footballing cows come home. As a start, in 2002 FIFA conducted a poll of more than a million fans to find the 'World Cup dream team', with Maradona topping the poll on 111,035 votes, followed by Pelé and Zidane. Here's that attack-minded dream team, with a bench of subs who might just as easily make the side. The only proviso is for players to have ended their international careers – so no Messi or Ronaldo. Let the debate begin …

LEV YASHIN	**PAOLO MALDINI**	**FRANZ BECKENBAUER**	**ROBERTO CARLOS**	**ROBERTO BAGGIO**	**ZINEDINE ZIDANE**
Goalkeeper	*Right back*	*Centre back/sweeper*	*Left back*	*Attacking midfielder*	*Attacking midfielder*
SOVIET UNION	ITALY	WEST GERMANY	BRAZIL	ITALY	FRANCE
1958, 1962, 1966, 1970	1990, 1994, 1998, 2002	1966, 1970, 1974	1998, 2002, 2006	1990, 1994, 1998	1998, 2002, 2006
78 caps	126 caps	103 caps	125 caps	56 caps	108 caps
13 World Cup matches	23 World Cup matches	18 World Cup matches	17 World Cup matches	16 World Cup matches	12 World Cup matches
		5 World Cup goals	1 World Cup goal	9 World Cup goals	5 World Cup goals

SUPER SUBSTITUTES

DINO ZOFF	**DJALMA SANTOS**	**BOBBY MOORE**	**NÍLTON SANTOS**	**FRANK RIJKAARD**	**XAVI**
Goalkeeper	*Right back*	*Centre back/sweeper*	*Left back*	*Defensive midfielder*	*Midfielder*
ITALY	BRAZIL	ENGLAND	BRAZIL	NETHERLANDS	SPAIN
1970, 1974, 1978, 1982	1954, 1958, 1962, 1966	1962, 1966, 1970	1950, 1954, 1958, 1962	1990, 1994	2002, 2006, 2010, 2014
112 caps	98 caps	108 caps	75 caps	73 caps	133 caps
17 World Cup matches	12 World Cup matches	14 World Cup matches	15 World Cup matches	8 World Cup matches	15 World Cup matches
	1 World Cup goal		1 World Cup goal		

MICHEL PLATINI

Attacking midfielder
FRANCE
1978, 1982, 1986
72 caps
14 World Cup matches
5 World Cup goals

DIEGO MARADONA

Attacking midfielder
ARGENTINA
1982, 1986, 1990, 1994
91 caps
21 World Cup matches
8 World Cup goals

PELÉ

Forward
BRAZIL
1958, 1962, 1966, 1970
91 caps
14 World Cup matches
12 World Cup goals

JOHAN CRUYFF

Forward
NETHERLANDS
1974
48 caps
7 World Cup matches
3 World Cup goals

ROMÁRIO

Forward
BRAZIL
1990, 1994
70 caps
8 World Cup matches
5 World Cup goals

WORLD CUP ABSENTEES

ALFREDO DI STÉFANO

GEORGE BEST

BERND SCHUSTER

RYAN GIGGS

GEORGE WEAH

ERIC CANTONA

LÁSZLÓ KUBALA

ZICO

Attacking midfielder
BRAZIL
1978, 1982, 1986
71 caps
14 World Cup matches
5 World Cup goals

BOBBY CHARLTON

Attacking midfielder
ENGLAND
1958, 1962, 1966, 1970
105 caps
14 World Cup matches
4 World Cup goals

GARRINCHA

Forward
BRAZIL
1958, 1962, 1966
50 caps
12 World Cup matches
5 World Cup goals

GERD MÜLLER

Forward
WEST GERMANY
1970, 1974
62 caps
13 World Cup matches
14 World Cup goals

FERENC PUSKÁS

Forward
HUNGARY
1954, 1962
84 caps
6 World Cup matches
4 World Cup goals

CHAMPIONS LEAGUE THRILLERS

The final of the European Cup – the Champions League from 1992 – has provided many memorable games. Three stand out, though, as perhaps the greatest of them all, including the deadliest football strikeforce ever assembled, the most breathtaking last-minute turnaround and the bravest comeback.

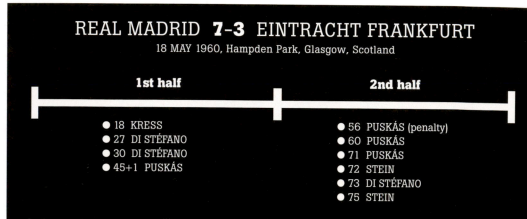

REAL MADRID **7-3** EINTRACHT FRANKFURT
18 MAY 1960, Hampden Park, Glasgow, Scotland

1st half

- 18 KRESS
- 27 DI STÉFANO
- 30 DI STÉFANO
- 45+1 PUSKÁS

2nd half

- 56 PUSKÁS (penalty)
- 60 PUSKÁS
- 71 PUSKÁS
- 72 STEIN
- 73 DI STÉFANO
- 75 STEIN

In the stands, among a record European final crowd of 127,621, was an 18-year-old Alex Ferguson, then a striker with Queen's Park. He witnessed a demolition of a good Eintracht Frankfurt side by Real Madrid, a team at its peak, having already won four successive European titles and featuring perhaps the finest frontline put out by any football club – Ferenc Puskás, Alfredo Di Stéfano and Francisco Gento. Eintracht actually opened the scoring on 18 minutes through Richard Kress, but by the time the Germans had managed a second, after 72 minutes, Real had already clocked up six goals, including four from Puskás. He and Di Stéfano, who scored a hat-trick, were irresistible, ably abetted by the creativity of Gento and midfielder Luis del Sol. As Puskás boasted, 'Every man in our team is an attacker.'

MANCHESTER UTD **2-1** BAYERN MUNICH
26 MAY 1999, Camp Nou, Barcelona, Spain

1st half

- 6 BASLER

2nd half

- 90:36 SHERINGHAM
- 92:17 SOLSKÆR

The final three minutes of the final Champions League of the twentieth century produced possibly the most exciting finish in the history of the competition. Manchester United, the first English team to appear in the final for nearly 15 years, had already won the double of league title and FA Cup, and now looked for a first-ever 'treble'. In the way were fellow treble-seekers Bayern, who took an early lead through a Mario Basler free kick and hit the woodwork twice. The Germans seemed in control, but in injury time Teddy Sheringham scrambled a scrappy equalizer from a corner, and then with seconds to go Ole Gunnar Solskjær poked home a close-range winner. 'Football, bloody hell' was Alex Ferguson's dazed reaction.

MIRACLE OF ISTANBUL

25 MAY 2005, Atatürk Olympic Stadium

AC MILAN 3-3 LIVERPOOL

Penalty shoot-out:
AC MILAN 2-3 LIVERPOOL

1st half	2nd half	Extra time

1st half
- 1 MALDINI
- 39 CRESPO
- 44 CRESPO

2nd half
- 54 GERRARD
- 56 ŠMICER
- 60 ALONSO

Penalties

AC MILAN			LIVERPOOL
SERGINHO	✗	●	HAMANN
PIRLO	✗	●	CISSÉ
TOMASSON	●	✗	RIISE
KAKÁ	●	●	ŠMICER
SHEVCHENKO	✗		

Paolo Maldini's first-minute goal quickly underlined AC Milan's supposed superiority over Liverpool. Two more goals just before half-time from Milan striker Hernán Crespo just about nailed the lid on the Scousers' coffin.

Come the second half, it looked all over, until a certain Steven Gerrard scored for Liverpool to spark a remarkable spell of three goals in six minutes and take the game into extra time. A tense 30 minutes produced no more goals – it was time for penalties. Liverpool's nerve held, while Milan's cracked, victory coming when goalkeeper Jerzy Dudek saved Andriy Shevchenko's spot kick. The English club's fightback, one of the most thrilling ever seen, was rightly named the 'Miracle of Istanbul'.

MAN OF THE MATCH
STEVEN GERRARD

8

103

WOMEN WORLD RULERS

In 1988, FIFA held an international women's football tournament in China to test the appetite for a regular global competition. It was a big enough success to encourage the launch of the Women's World Cup in 1991 – 61 years after the first men's World Cup. Crowds, interest and prize money continue to grow, with 1.3 million spectators attending matches at the 2015 World Cup in Canada, and more expected at the 2019 tournament in France. The USA has won three finals and leads the world rankings, followed by Germany.

352
Number of caps won by Kristine Lilly of USA, 1987–2010 – she also scored 130 international goals

1991 CHINA Teams 12
Final
USA 2–1 NORWAY

1995 SWEDEN Teams 12
Final
NORWAY 2–0 GERMANY

1999 UNITED STATES Teams 16
Final
USA 0–0 CHINA PR (a.e.t.)
(5–4 penalties)

2003 UNITED STATES Teams 16
Final
GERMANY 2–1 SWEDEN
(win on Golden Goal)

2007 CHINA PR Teams 16
Final
GERMANY 2–0 BRAZIL

2011 GERMANY Teams 16
Final
JAPAN 2–2 USA (a.e.t.)
(3–1 penalties)

2015 CANADA Teams 24
Final
USA 5–2 JAPAN

40

Age of Christie Rampone of the USA at the 2015 World Cup, making her the oldest woman to play in the final

7

7 countries in Europe have more than 60,000 registered women players:

England, France, Norway, Sweden, Denmark, Netherlands and Germany

1.2 million

Number of registered women players within the 54 European football associations of UEFA in 2015 – that's 0.3 per cent of all women in Europe

25,664

Average attendance for matches at the 2015 Women's World Cup – at the 1999 tournament the average was 19,615

90,185

Attendance at the 1999 World Cup final at the Rose Bowl, Pasadena, USA, the biggest-ever crowd at a women's sporting event

20%

In the US, nearly 20 per cent of all high-school female athletes – **around 375,000** – play football, making up 47 per cent of all women football players in the US

Football

has overtaken baseball and softball in the US to become the third-most-played high-school female sport, after basketball and volleyball

127

Number of countries listed in the FIFA world women's football rankings in early 2017 – in 1971, there were three national women's football teams and only two international matches played in that year

The number of women players in Europe has grown 5 times since 1985

BEND IT LIKE BECKHAM

The crowd holds its breath, the wall and keeper are in position, and a player waits over the ball, weighing up his options. Nothing beats the heightened anticipation before a free kick. Will it be a spectacular strike, or a damp squib? The scorer of great dead-ball goals is a priceless assest to any team – and few have been more valuable than these practitioners of the art.

JUNINHO PERNAMBUCANO
1993–2013

Often hailed as the greatest free-kick taker of all, the Brazilian midfielder perfected the art of 'knuckle–balling' – hitting through the ball with power but minimal spin to make its trajectory more unpredicatable. Of the 100 goals he scored for Olympique Lyonnais (2001–09), 44 were free kicks, some from seemingly impossible distances, up to 40m (130ft) from the target. Those goals helped the French club to seven successive Ligue 1 titles.

CRISTIANO RONALDO
2002–

Like Pernambucano, Ronaldo has learnt how to hit a mean 'knuckle-ball', generating a tremendous amount of force. The Real Madrid and Portugal player has been known to use this ability to whip the ball straight at the goal, under the wall as the defenders jump.

ROBERTO CARLOS
1991–2015

No player hit a free kick harder – or with a longer run–up – than Brazilian Carlos. But it was not just about power. In a 1997 match against France, he struck a free kick from 35m (115ft) out, bending it so far that a ball boy 10m (33ft) to the right of the goal ducked, before the ball curled back inside the post.

ANDREA PIRLO

1995–

Former Italy coach Marcello Lippi once said, 'Pirlo … speaks with his feet,' and that's eactly what the elegant midfielder has done repeatedly when taking a free kick. Like Siniša Mihajlović (see below), Pirlo scored 28 free kicks in Serie A, mostly for AC Milan and Juventus. The Italian has honed both a wickedly curling kick from close to the box that can bamboozle any goalkeeper and a powerful, swerving long-range blast.

DAVID BECKHAM

1992–2013

In the Premier League, Beckham converted 15 direct free kicks, more than any other player. He also scored the memorable last-gasp free kick against Greece that took England to the 2002 World Cup. Placement rather than power marked his kicking, with a precise approach and perfectly balanced body shape.

ZICO

1971–94

The Brazilian midfielder made it look so easy. A slight pause, hardly any run-up and a lazy delivery of the ball into whichever corner of the goal he chose. This took practice, though. After training, Zico would place a shirt in each top corner of the goal and repeatedly take them down from 20m (65ft).

SINIŠA MIHAJLOVIĆ

1986–2006

For sheer variety – close in, far out, piledrivers, curlers over the wall – it's hard to improve on the left-footed Serbian. He featured in Red Star Belgrade's European Cup victory in 1991 and spent 14 years in Serie A, where he became one of only two players to score a hat-trick of free kicks (for Lazio against Sampdoria in 1998) and reach a total of 28 league free kicks.

WORLD CUP SHOCKERS

There's nothing like a World Cup to put some fizz into so-called underdogs, induce complacency in the hotly tipped or simply tear up the form book. Big shocks don't come along every day, but when they do they are moments to be savoured – unless you support the team disappearing down a hole.

BELITTLED IN BELO HORIZONTE

BRAZIL **1–7** GERMANY

8 July 2014, Estádio Mineirão, Belo Horizonte, Brazil

1st half

- 11 MÜLLER
- 23 KLOSE
- 24 KROOS
- 26 KROOS
- 29 KHEDIRA

2nd half

- 69 SCHÜRRLE
- 79 SCHÜRRLE
- 90 OSCAR

Brazil, as the host nation, and with the most passionate supporters in the world, were expected to go all the way to the final, despite losing their star striker, Neymar, to injury. Germany were going to be a tough test, but no one expected them to roll the Brazilians over with such ease. The humiliation was total, including four goals scored in six blink-and-you'll-miss-it minutes.

CAMEROON **1–0** ARGENTINA

8 June 1990, Milan, Italy

1st half   **2nd half**

- 67 OMAM-BIYIK

Cameroon were making only their second appearance in a World Cup and were expected to be easy meat for Argentina, the reigning world champions. Despite being reduced to 10 men on 61 minutes, Cameroon scored through striker François Omam-Biyik, then miraculously held out after a second player was sent off in the closing minutes.

NORTH KOREA **1–0** ITALY

19 July 1966, Middlesbrough, England

1st half   **2nd half**

- 42 PAK DOO IK

As the tournament began, North Korea, which didn't even have diplomatic relations with the hosts, were 1000-1 outsiders, while two-time World Cup winners Italy were expected to trounce the Asians. Army corporal Pak Doo Ik had different ideas and fired his team into a lead they clung on to valiantly. In the quarterfinals, the Koreans took an even more unlikely 3-0 lead against Portugal, until Eusébio inspired a five-goal Portuguese comeback.

THE NEARLY MAN
JOHAN CRUYFF *Netherlands*
Cruyff and his Dutch team of 'total' footballers were
unstoppable on their march to the 1974 World Cup final,
but somehow managed to lose. It was a shock, as was Cruyff's
non-appearance at the 1978 World Cup having led his country
all the way through the qualifiers.

SALVADOR
SMASH-AND-GRAB

SPAIN **1–5** NETHERLANDS
13 June 2014, Arena Fonte Nova, Salvador, Brazil

1st half	2nd half
● 27 ALONSO (pen.)	● 53 ROBBEN
● 44 VAN PERSIE	● 72 VAN PERSIE
	● 83 DE VRIJ
	● 80 ROBBEN

Reigning world champions and former
underachievers Spain were taking on perennial
disappointments the Netherlands. It was going
to be a close call, and it all looked like normal
service for Spain when Xabi Alonso converted
a penalty on 27 minutes. Then, as half-time
approached, Robin van Persie scored one of
the greatest headers of all time, the Dutchmen
regrouped and then went on to slaughter the
dazed and confused Spanish in the second half.

SHAMED BY THE STATES

USA **1–0** ENGLAND
29 June 1950, Estádio Independência, Belo Horizonte, Brazil

1st half	2nd half
● 38 GAETJENS	

This was only the first World Cup that England had entered. They were, though, considered one of the
mostly likely teams to win the tournament and overwhelming favourites to steamroller the United States'
part-timers. In the event, England suffered their most embarrassing defeat, undone by a goal from Joe
Gaetjens, a Haitian studying accountancy in New York. Gaetjens later played one game for Haiti.

LA LIGA ... BY THE NUMBERS

Spain's Primera División, or La Liga, began in 1929, with just ten teams and Barcelona champions. It has grown into Europe's strongest league – 20 sides, each playing 38 games and attracting many of the world's greatest players, such as Messi, Neymar and Ronaldo. Real Madrid and Barcelona have dominated the league for the past decade, with only Atlético Madrid breaking their stranglehold in 2013–14.

550
League appearances for Real Madrid by Raúl (1994–2010) – the most for one club

3
Number of clubs that have played in every La Liga season: Real Madrid, Barcelona, Athletic Bilbao

121
Goals scored in one season by Real Madrid (2011–12) – the record

99,354
Capacity of Barcelona's Camp Nou stadium, the largest in Spain

32
Most wins in a season – Real Madrid (2011–12), Barcelona (2012–13)

12–1
Biggest victory in La Liga history, Athletic Bilbao v Barcelona, 1931

5
Number of titles Real Madrid won in succession, 1961–65 and 1986–90

757
Number of La Liga games in which Luis Aragonés managed a team (1974–2004)

50
League goals scored by Lionel Messi of Barcelona in 2011–12 season, at an average of 1.316 goals per match

9
Number of clubs that have won La Liga:
Real Madrid **32**
Barcelona **24**
Atlético Madrid **10**
Athletic Bilbao **8**
Valencia **6**
Real Sociedad **2**
Deportivo La Coruña **1**
Sevilla **1**
Real Betis **1**

16 YEARS 98 DAYS
Age of Fabrice Olinga, youngest goalscorer in the league – Málaga v Celta Vigo, 18 August 2012

252
Goal tally reached on 22 November 2014 by Lionel Messi in his 289th league game when he netted the second of three goals against Sevilla – overtaking Athletic Bilbao's Telmo Zarra (1940–55) to become La Liga's highest goalscorer

622
Record La Liga appearances, made by Andoni Zubizarreta (1981–98), who also won 126 caps for Spain

12
Record number of league winners medals, won by Francisco Gento, all for Real Madrid (1954–69)

SERIE A ... BY THE NUMBERS

Like La Liga, Italy's national football league started life, in its present format, in 1929 and has 20 teams each playing 38 games across a season. The Serie A title is also known as the Scudetto, named after the small shield worn on the shirts of the team that hold the title.

5

Number of consecutive titles won by Internazionale between 2005–06 and 2009–10

102

Record number of points won in the 2013–14 season by Juventus, who also won a record 33 out of 38 matches

44 YEARS 38 DAYS

Age of Lazio goalkeeper Marco Ballotta when he played his final Serie A game in 2008

1897

Year that Juventus, the oldest club in Serie A, was founded in Turin

58

Number of games AC Milan went unbeaten between 1990 and 1993

2

Titles stripped from Juventus (2004–05 and 2005–06) for their involvement in the Calciopoli match-rigging scandal

929

Minutes that AC Milan goalkeeper Sebastiano Rossi played without conceding a goal in the 1993–94 season

80,018

Capacity of the Stadio Giuseppe Meazza, or San Siro, in Milan, the largest Serie A stadium and home to AC Milan and Internazionale

85

Number of seasons Internazionale has appeared in Serie A, more than any other team

274

Record number of Serie A goals, scored by Silvio Piola, 1929–54

11

Number of Serie A clubs managed by Alberto Malesani – Fiorentina, Parma, Verona, Modena, Udinese, Empoli, Siena, Bologna, Genoa, Palermo, Sassuolo

12

Clubs that have won the title (since 1929):
Juventus **30**
Internazionale **16**
AC Milan **15**
Torino **6**
Bologna **5**
AS Roma **3**
Fiorentina **2**
Lazio **2**
Napoli **2**
Cagliari **1**
Verona **1**
Sampdoria **1**

647

Record number of appearances in Serie A for Paolo Maldini (1985–2009), all for AC Milan

ACTION!

They may show plenty of acting prowess on the pitch, but most footballers are not renowned for their abilities in front of a camera. Some, though, have made the leap from the big match to the big screen. Cue these ten memorable and less-than-memorable soccer thespians.

PAUL BREITNER
48 caps West Germany

Played Sergeant Stark in German 'Western' *Potato Fritz* (1976)

FRANK LEBŒUF
50 caps France

8 feature films, including a Swiss doctor in **The Theory of Everything** (2014) and a French resistance fighter in **Allies** (2014)

VINNIE JONES
9 caps Wales

More than **60** film roles, including Big Chris in **Lock, Stock and Two Smoking Barrels** (1998), Bullet-Tooth Tony in **Snatch** (2000) and the voice of Freddie the Dog in **Madagascar 3** (2012)

PELÉ
91 caps Brazil

10 feature films, including **Escape to Victory** (1981) and **A Minor Miracle** (1983)

NICOLAS ANELKA
69 caps France

Typecast as Nicolas, a football player, in **Dead Weight** (2002)

ÉRIC CANTONA
45 caps France

More than **20** film parts, including Monsieur de Foix in *Elizabeth* (1998) and himself in *Looking for Eric* (2009)

GEOFF HURST
49 caps England

Played football agent Adam Avely in *Payback Season* (2012)

DAVID BECKHAM
115 caps England

Cameo roles in *The Man from U.N.C.L.E.* (2015) and *King Arthur: Legend of the Sword* (2017)

DAVID GINOLA
17 caps France

Played Corporal Dieter Max in *The Last Drop* (2006)

ALLY McCOIST
61 caps Scotland

Played footballer Jackie McQuillan opposite Robert Duvall as his team manager in *A Shot at Glory* (2000)

★ **17** ★

The number of present and former professional footballers who appeared in *Escape to Victory* (1981), including Pelé, Bobby Moore and Osvaldo Ardiles, and no fewer than seven players from the squad of Ipswich Town: Paul Cooper, Kevin Beattie, Laurie Sivell, Russell Osman, John Wark, Kevin O'Callaghan and Robin Turner.

THERE ARE PEOPLE ON THE PITCH …

Football is a simple sport, making it easy for fans to play the game, too – or get involved as a referee or other official. According to FIFA research, 265 million people worldwide play football and another 5 million officiate – that's 4 per cent of our planet's popluation. Here are the countries that top the participation charts.

REGISTERED PLAYERS

These are the pros and amateurs registered in the top 8 participating countries.
Figures in millions

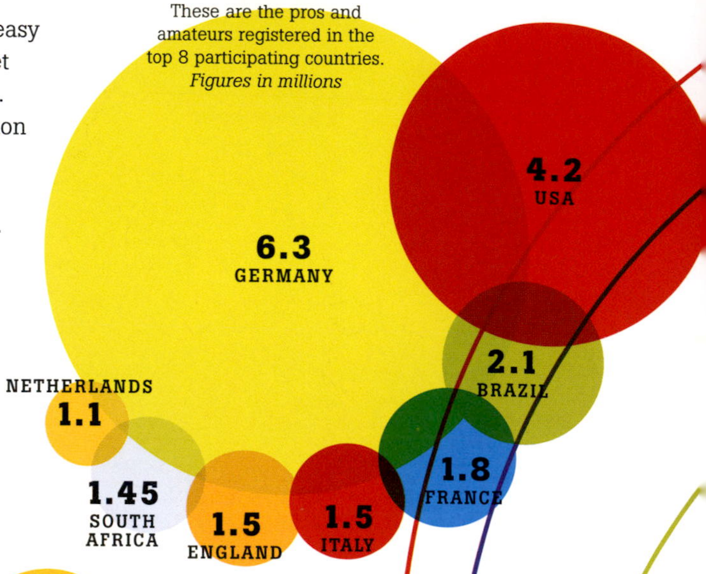

4.2
USA

6.3
GERMANY

2.1
BRAZIL

1.8
FRANCE

NETHERLANDS
1.1

1.45
SOUTH AFRICA

1.5
ENGLAND

1.5
ITALY

OFFICIALS

Referees, assistant referees, club officers and others who run and rule the game – the top 8 countries.
Figures in thousands

796.3
USA

392.8
AUSTRIA

208.0
TURKEY

310.6
ETHIOPIA

249.6
JAPAN

285.7
FRANCE

257.8
SWITZERLAND

259.8
RUSSIA

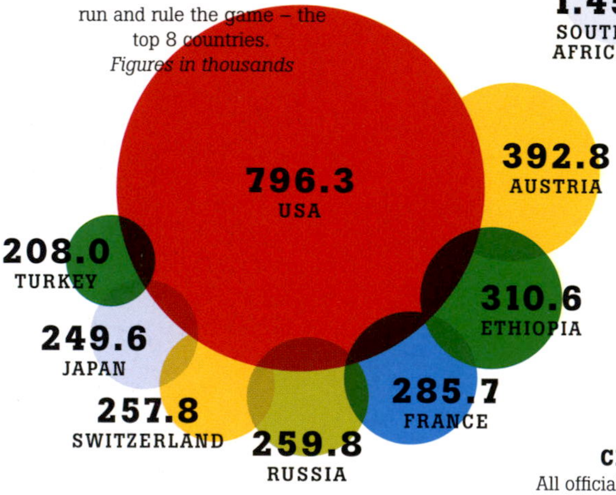

CLUBS

All officially recognized professional and amateur league clubs – the top 8 countries.
Figures in thousands

10.0
CANADA

42.5
ENGLAND

29.2
BRAZIL

14.3
RUSSIA

16.7
ITALY

18.2
SPAIN

20.0
FRANCE

26.8
GERMANY

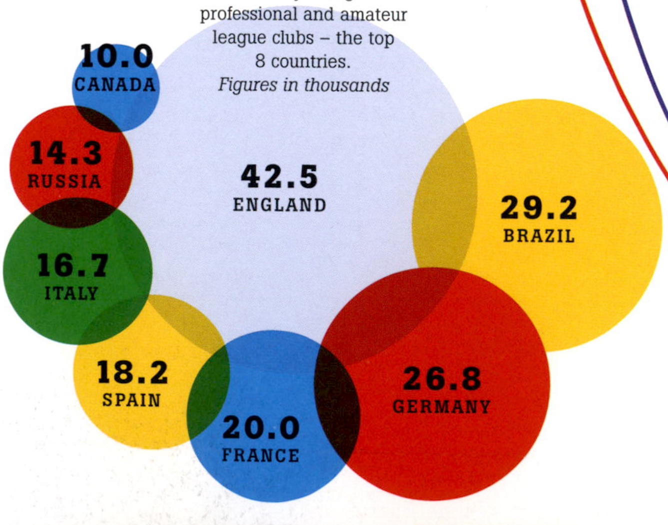

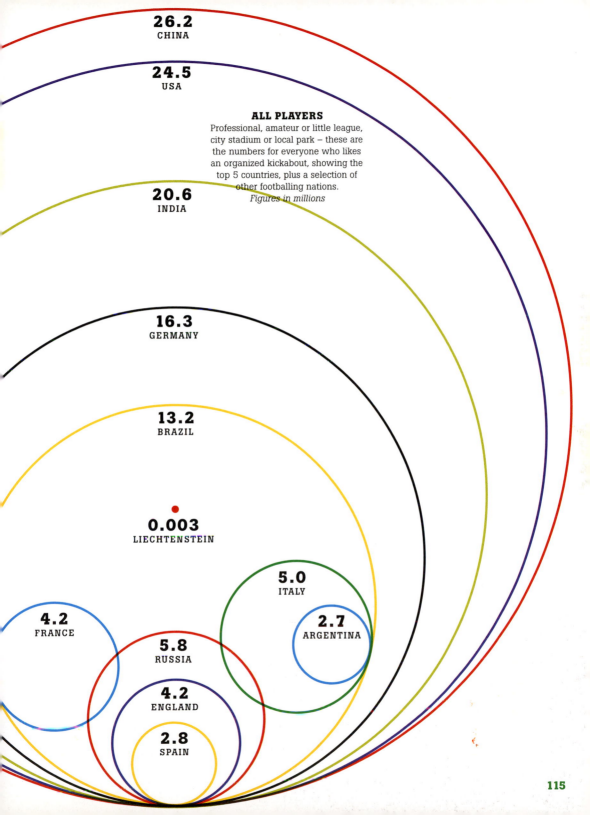

26.2
CHINA

24.5
USA

ALL PLAYERS
Professional, amateur or little league,
city stadium or local park – these are
the numbers for everyone who likes
an organized kickabout, showing the
top 5 countries, plus a selection of
other footballing nations.
Figures in millions

20.6
INDIA

16.3
GERMANY

13.2
BRAZIL

0.003
LIECHTENSTEIN

5.0
ITALY

4.2
FRANCE

2.7
ARGENTINA

5.8
RUSSIA

4.2
ENGLAND

2.8
SPAIN

GIANTS OF THE WORLD

They may not have the global pulling power of a Real Madrid or Manchester United, but the most successful clubs in the Americas, Asia and Africa are just as important to their own passionate fans. Take a quick grand tour of some of the world's champion teams.

1

LA GALAXY
Founded 1996
★
MLS Cup **5**
Supporters' Shield **4**
CONCACAF
Champions League **1**

2

D.C. UNITED
Founded 1995
★
MLS Cup **4**
Supporters' Shield **4**
CONCACAF
Champions League **1**

3

BOCA JUNIORS
Founded 1905
★
League titles **31**
Copa Argentina **3**
Copa Libertadores **6**

4

RIVER PLATE
Founded 1901
★
League titles **36**
Copa Campeonato **1**
Copa Libertadores **3**

5

CLUB AMÉRICA
Founded 1916
★
League titles **16**
Copa México/MX **6**
CONCACAF
Champions League **7**

6

FLAMENGO
Founded 1895
★
League titles **5**
Copa do Brasil **3**
Copa Libertadores **1**

7

**CD GUADALAJARA
(CHIVAS)**
Founded 1906
★
League titles **11**
Copa México/MX **3**
CONCACAF
Champions League **1**

8

SANTOS
Founded 1912
★
League titles **8**
Copa do Brasil **1**
Copa Libertadores **3**

9

SÃO PAULO
Founded 1930
★
League titles **6**
Copa Libertadores **3**
FIFA Club World
Cup **1**

10

PALMEIRAS
Founded 1914
★
League titles **9**
Copa do Brasil **3**
Copa Libertadores **1**

11 PEÑAROL
Founded 1891
★
League titles **48**
Copa Libertadores **5**
South American Club of
the Century (2009)

12 SEONGNAM FC
Founded 1989
★
League titles **7**
Korean FA Cup **3**
AFC Champions
League **2**

13 GUANGZHOU
EVERGRANDE
Founded 1954
★
League titles **6**
Chinese FA Cup **2**
AFC Champions
League **2**

14 AL-HILAL
Founded 1957
★
League titles **13**
King Cup **7**
AFC Champions
League **2**

15 AL SADD
Founded 1969
★
League titles **13**
Emir of Qatar Cup **15**
AFC Champions
League **2**

16 KAIZER CHIEFS
Founded 1970
★
League titles **4**
MTN 8 Cup **15**
CAF Confederations
Cup **1**

17 AL AHLY
Founded 1907
★
League titles **38**
Egypt Cup **35**
CAF Champions
League **8**

18 ESPÉRANCE
DE TUNIS
Founded 1919
★
League titles **26**
Tunisian Cup **15**
CAF Champions
League **2**

19 RAJA
CASABLANCA
Founded 1949
★
League titles **11**
Moroccan Cup **7**
CAF Champions
League **3**

20 TP MAZEMBE
Founded 1939
★
League titles **15**
Coupe du Congo **5**
CAF Champions
League **5**

FOOTBALL GOES EAST

Asia has the second-oldest continental tournament, after South America's Copa América. The Asian Football Confederation established the AFC Asian Cup in 1956, and it has been held every four years since, except for a switch in 2007 to avoid a clash with other tournaments. A small number of countries have dominated the finals, with Australia (a non–Asian participant since 2007) the winner in 2015.

AFC ASIAN CUP

	HOST	WINNER	RUNNER-UP
1956	Hong Kong	South Korea	Israel
1960	South Korea	South Korea	Israel
1964	Israel	Israel	India
1968	Iran	Iran	Burma
1972	Thailand	Iran	South Korea
1976	Iran	Iran	Kuwait
1980	Kuwait	Kuwait	South Korea
1984	Singapore	Saudi Arabia	China PR
1988	Qatar	Saudi Arabia	South Korea
1992	Japan	Japan	Saudi Arabia
1996	United Arab Emirates	Saudi Arabia	United Arab Emirates
2000	Lebanon	Japan	Saudi Arabia
2004	China PR	Japan	China PR
2007	Indonesia/Malaysia/ Thailand/Vietnam	Iraq	Saudi Arabia
2011	Qatar	Japan	Australia
2015	Australia	Australia	South Korea

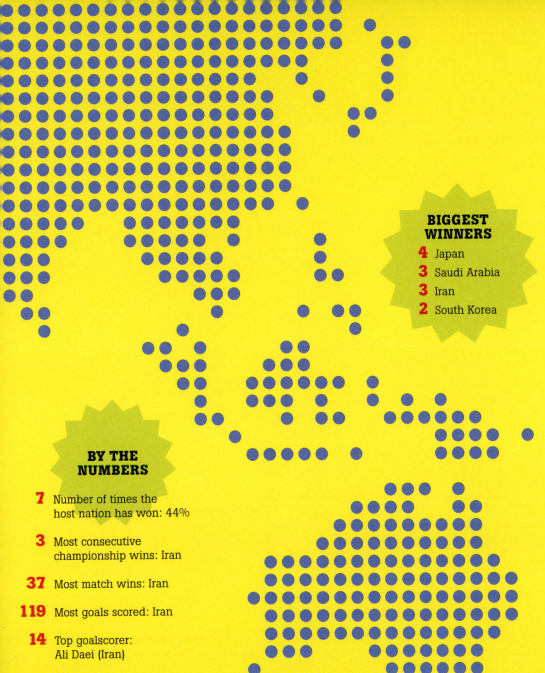

BIGGEST WINNERS

4 Japan

3 Saudi Arabia

3 Iran

2 South Korea

BY THE NUMBERS

7 Number of times the host nation has won: 44%

3 Most consecutive championship wins: Iran

37 Most match wins: Iran

119 Most goals scored: Iran

14 Top goalscorer: Ali Daei (Iran)

8–0 Biggest victory: Iran 8–0 South Yemen 1976

9 Most goals in a match: Japan 8–1 Uzbekistan 2000

DEMANDING? MOI?

We know about the strange and extreme demands made by film stars and pop divas on set or on tour. But footballers and their entourages can be just as picky, from commandeering gyms and swimming pools to stipulating the exact source of a banana. Take a look at these fussy non-negotiables from the 2014 World Cup.

ENGLAND

- ☑ exclusive use of one hotel restaurant
- ☑ video games room with three TVs and the most up-to-date games
- ☑ exclusive use of the gym and swimming pool for a few hours each day
- ☑ two floors of 64 rooms reserved by squad and technical staff
- ☑ total cost to hotel: more than £2 million, including new beds, wooden floors, rust-free balconies and air-conditioning

USA

- ☑ fresh fruit and honey cake every day as a dessert
- ☑ meals cooked by Michelin-starred Spanish chef Sergi Arola

AUSTRALIA

- ☑ coffee machines for four players
- ☑ newspapers from around the world
- ☑ Brazilian meals of red meat, fish and chicken

CHILE

- ☑ new bed and flatscreen TV in each room

FRANCE

- ☑ every player's room to be identical, including the same colour
- ☑ two different types of liquid soap: one for showering, one for hand-washing
- ☑ halal meat only

JAPAN

- ☑ a Jacuzzi in each room

COSTA RICA

- ☑ large chill-out room with sofas, TVs and video games

ECUADOR

- ☑ fresh supply of bananas every day, sourced only from Ecuador
- ☑ welcome barbecue

URUGUAY

- ☑ totally silent air-conditioning units

BOSNIA

- ☑ soundproofed screen, so players can dine on one side and coaching staff on the other

GERMANY

- ☑ purpose-built training centre
- ☑ gated team HQ, with 13 houses, 65 rooms, a football field and a press centre

COLOMBIA

- ☑ 15 players from the São Paulo youth team to practise against

SWITZERLAND

- ☑ beach studio for TV interviews
- ☑ two Swiss TV channels in each room

IRAN

- ☑ free dry-cleaning

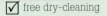

PORTUGAL

- ☑ six bodyguards, four of them for Cristiano Ronaldo
- ☑ video games in each room

ALGERIA

- ☑ a copy of the Koran beside each bed

PENALTY BOX TO SOAP BOX

Footballers are not always known as the brightest of sparks, usually more interested in cars, nightclubs and kitting out their mansions than they are in public transport, employment rates or affordable housing. So it may come as a surprise to find players who have made the unlikely move from pitch to politics. Please be upstanding for this electable XI.

ROMAN PAVLYUCHENKO
Council deputy

★ 51 caps for Russia (2003–13), 141 league appearances for Spartak Moscow and 78 league games for Tottenham Hotspur

★ Elected as a deputy on the regional council for his home town of Stavropol in 2008, standing for Vladimir Putin's United Russia party

ROMÁRIO
Senator

★ 70 caps for Brazil (1987–2005), 55 goals – only Pelé and Ronaldo have scored more for Brazil – and member of the winning team in the 1994 World Cup final

★ Elected to the Chamber of Deputies at the 2010 general election as Brazilian Socialist Party candidate

★ Elected to Brazilian senate in 2014 general election

OLEH BLOKHIN
MP

★ 112 caps and 42 goals for the Soviet Union (1972–88), more than 400 league appearances for Dynamo Kiev

★ Elected to the Ukranian parliament in 1998 and 2002

HAKAN ŞÜKÜR
MP

★ 112 caps and 51 goals for Turkey (1992–2007), more than 500 league appearances in total for seven clubs in Europe, including Galatasaray, Parma and Blackburn Rovers

★ Scored fastest goal in World Cup history – 10.8 seconds in third-place play-off with South Korea in 2002

★ Elected as MP for the Justice and Development Party in the 2011 Turkish general election

★ Resigned from the ruling party in 2013 and continued as an independent MP, losing his seat in 2015

GEORGE WEAH
Senator

★ 60 caps and 22 goals for Liberia (1987–2007), more than 100 appearances for both Monaco and AC Milan, 1995 FIFA World Player of the Year

★ Ran for Liberian presidency in 2005, and in 2016 announced his intention to run again

★ Elected to Liberian Senate in 2014

TITI CAMARA
Sports Minister

★ 38 caps and 23 goals for Guinea (1992–2004), more than 350 league games for Liverpool, Saint-Étienne, Lens, Marseille and others

★ Appointed Guinea sports minister in 2010

GIANNI RIVERA
MP & MEP

★ 63 caps and 15 goals for Italy (1962–75), 501 league appearances for AC Milan, winner of the Ballon d'Or, 1969
★ Elected as an Italian MP from 1987 to 2001
★ Junior minister for defence in four different Italian governments, 1996–2001
★ MEP, 2005–09

BEBETO
State legislator

★ 75 caps and 39 goals for Brazil (1985–98), 131 league appearances for Deportivo La Coruña, member of World Cup winning team in 1994
★ Elected onto Rio's state legislature in 2010, representing the Democratic Workers' Party

GRZEGORZ LATO
Senator

★ 100 caps and 45 goals for Poland (1971–84), top scorer at 1974 World Cup with 7 goals
★ Served as senator in Polish parliament, 2001–05, for Democratic Left Alliance

MARC WILMOTS
Senator

★ 70 caps and 28 goals for Belgium (1990–2002), more than 100 league appearances for Standard Liège and Schalke 04, manager of Belgium national team 2012–
★ Elected to the Belgium senate in 2003, representing the French-speaking liberal party, The Reformist Movement

YORDAN LETCHKOV
Mayor

★ 45 caps and 5 goals for Bulgaria (1989–98), including the winning header against Germany in the quarterfinal of the 1994 World Cup
★ Elected mayor of his home town, Sliven, in 2003, and again in 2007
★ Sentenced to two years in prison in 2013 for corruption

And last but not least …

PELÉ
UN Ambassador, Minister for Sport, humanitarian and environmental campaigner

★ 91 caps and 77 goals for Brazil (1957–71) and just about the world's best-loved player
★ Made an honorary Knight Commander of the British Empire in 1997

PLEASE, ALLOW ME …

Goals win matches, and it is often the goal scorers who grab the glory. But of equal, if not greater, value is the player whose pass, cross or knock-back creates the opportunity for a team-mate to score. These 'assists' are recorded as avidly as actual goals, and certain players in the biggest European leagues tower above all others for their ability to create scoring opportunities.

MESUT ÖZIL
Arsenal, Real Madrid and Germany

He may lag behind a certain Mr Messi in terms of total assists but Mesut Özil had a superior 'pass success' rate stretching over five seasons, 2010–15 – 86 per cent against 85.8 per cent. It may not be much, but Özil is probably one of the few, if any, players who can say he has surpassed the little genius at any aspect of the playmaker's art.

Goal-making assists 2010–15
5 seasons • League and Champions League

LIONEL MESSI
Barcelona
75 La Liga, 15 Champions League

MESUT ÖZIL
Arsenal, Real Madrid
61 Premier League/La Liga, 16 Champions League

CRISTIANO RONALDO
Real Madrid
58 La Liga, 15 Champions League

ÁNGEL DI MARIA
Manchester United, Real Madrid (now Paris Saint-Germain)
59 Premier League/La Liga, 13 Champions League

CESC FÀBREGAS
Chelsea, Barcelona, Arsenal
60 Premier League/La Liga, 9 Champions League

FRANCK RIBÉRY
Bayern Munich
54 Bundesliga, 10 Champions League

KARIM BENZEMA
Real Madrid
42 La Liga, 16 Champions League

EDEN HAZARD
Chelsea, Lille
53 Premier League/Ligue 1, 5 Champions League

JUAN MATA
Manchester United, Chelsea, Valencia
47 Premier League/La Liga, 9 Champions League

ANDRÉS INIESTA
Barcelona
36 La Liga, 16 Champions League

DAVID SILVA
Manchester City
46 Premier League, 4 Champions League

WAYNE ROONEY
Manchester United
40 Premier League, 10 Champions League

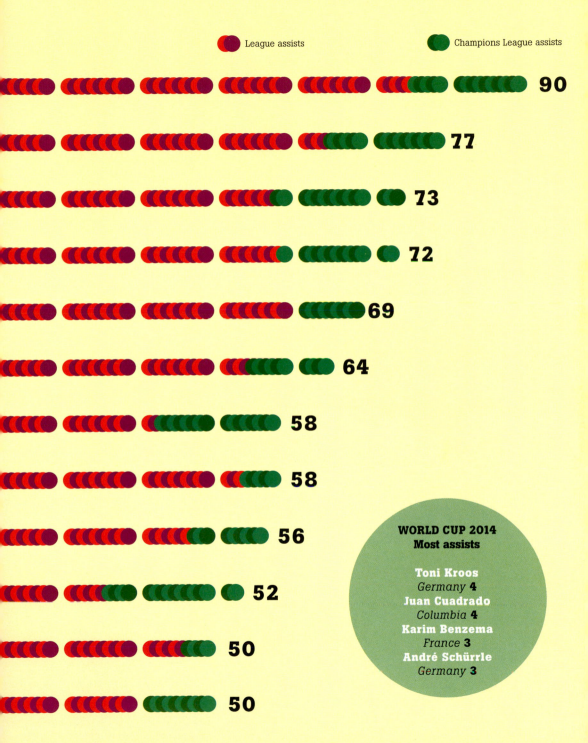

League assists   Champions League assists

90

77

73

72

69

64

58

58

56

52

50

50

WORLD CUP 2014
Most assists

Toni Kroos
Germany **4**
Juan Cuadrado
Columbia **4**
Karim Benzema
France **3**
André Schürrle
Germany **3**

CELEBRATION TIME

Goal! You've scored, you're very happy and feel the need to celebrate. In the old days, a simple nod and a handshake sufficed, but more recently footballers have injected dance, acrobatics, politics, family matters and sheer silliness into the act. There's no place for modesty here, but plenty of room for embarrassment.

The knee-slide

Almost the default post-score activity – easy on a wet pitch, comical when dry. A statue outside Arsenal's stadium shows Thierry Henry, a skilled slider, in the pose, but the celebration inventor is said to be Dragan Mance, a Partizan Belgrade striker in the early 1980s.

Head over heels

Beloved of African footballers, the backflip celebration was brought to the world stage by Nigerian striker Julius Aghahowa at the 2002 World Cup, when he did seven flips after scoring against Sweden.

Wiggle, wiggle, wiggle ...

Probably the most memorable celebration of all, Roger Milla's trademark corner flag 'wiggle' was performed after each of his four goals at the 1990 World Cup. Try it yourself:

1 First, score a goal

2 Head for the nearest corner flag

3 Stand in front of the flag, raise one hand, place the other on your stomach and

wiggle, wiggle, wiggle ...

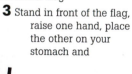

Headless chicken

A favourite with Mr Balotelli and many others, especially those with some words on their vest to share with the world, the shirt-pulled-over-the-head look was popularized by the grey-haired Italian striker Fabrizio Ravanelli in the 1990s.

Someone up there ...

Arms lifted, eyes raised and fingers pointing to the skies – it's now a common sight as a player dedicates a goal to the divine or to a departed loved one. The most memorable salute was Frank Lampard's emotional reaction after he scored the winning goal in the 2008 Champions League semifinal only days after his mother's death.

Rock the baby

The Brazilian striker Bebeto is to blame for this now standard celebration of a goal and fatherhood. He stood, proudly rocking his arms, as if cradling his newborn, after scoring in the quarterfinal of the 2004 World Cup.

Why always me?

Mario Balotelli is never far from controversy, and when better to ruffle a few feathers than after a goal? Adverse press coverage of his private life prompted his 'Why always me?' protest in 2011.

The dentist's chair

Bizarrely, following a genius goal from Paul 'Gazza' Gascoigne against Scotland at Euro 1996, some England players thought it would be a hoot to pour water into the scorer's mouth to re-enact the 'dentist's chair' drinking game they had enjoyed on a pre-tournament trip to a Hong Kong nightclub.

Taking a dive

Jürgen Klinsmann arrived at Tottenham Hotspur in 1994 with a reputation for diving. So, what did he do when he scored a goal in the opening game of the season? He unveiled the first dive-and-slide celebration, joined by his joyous team-mates.

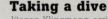

LONG JOHNS TO LYCRA

Woollen tops, long trousers and thick 'stockings' – spare a thought for 19th-century footballers and their uncomfortable kit. That combination soon evolved into the shirt, shorts and socks we know today, but in between, materials have changed, fashion has dictated new lengths, cuts and colours, and the football business has made big money from a simple set of clothes.

Early players grab what they can find, often what they might wear in another sport, such as cricket. Increasingly, clubs use colour, in blocks or hoops, to differentiate themselves, such as the dark blue and red 'jerseys' of the Royal Engineers (above).

Rules about covering knees are relaxed, and so 'knickers' become 'shorts'. Hoops and other detail appear on 'stockings', such as those of the Manchester United 1909 FA Cup team (above). Numbered shirts are first worn in the 1933 FA Cup final.

A new 'continental' style develops, with short sleeves, collarless V-neck shirts and shorter shorts, such as the kit worn by Manchester City at the 1956 FA Cup final (above). Man-made fabrics also emerge, including nylon, used in socks.

Shirts get tighter, shorts shorter, sleeves longer and colours lighter. Leeds United (above) change into white, partly to stand out under floodlights. In 1973, Eintracht Braunschweig of the Bundesliga become the first team to display a sponsor's name.

BRANDING TAKES OVER

Shirt sponsorship takes off in England, Germany and Italy. In 1982, Real Madrid are the first La Liga side to carry sponsorship (above). Lighter, less moisture-absorbent polyester takes over from cotton. This also allows more patterns and stronger colours.

Money floods into football, with TV deals, all-seater stadiums and replica shirts. Players' names appear for the first time, as does an excess of pattern and colour, as in the Borussia Dortmund kit worn in the 1997 Champions League final (above).

High-tech materials such as lycra are used to add strength and elasticity. Shirt designs become plainer and less cluttered, while more logos appear, including some to support events or charities, as on the 2013–14 AS Roma home shirt (above).

BOX TO BOX OFFICE

With the notable exceptions of boxing and baseball, sport has rarely translated well to the silver screen. No football movie has won an Oscar, but there have been some standout successes at the box office. Here are 10 that have scored big around the world.

Dollars = worldwide box office gross

MEAN MACHINE
2001 (UK)
$7,310,206

Danny 'Mean Machine' Meehan (**Vinnie Jones**) is an ex-England captain jailed for assault. In prison, he receives no favours but wins over the inmates and forms a team to take on the nasty prison guards.

SHAOLIN SOCCER
2001 (Hong Kong)
$42,776,760

Former football player 'Golden Leg' Fung (**Man Tat Ng**) meets Shaolin kung fu devotee 'Mighty Steel Leg' Sing (**Stephen Chow**) and the two form a soccer team, which enters a competition offering a $1 million prize. This gives Fung the chance to defeat Team Evil and Coach Hung, the man Fung blames for ending his playing career. It could happen …

BEND IT LIKE BECKHAM
2002 (UK)
$76,583,333

A London girl, Jess (**Parminder Nagra**), daughter of Punjabi parents, is spotted for her football skills by Jules (**Keira Knightley**) – star of the local Hounslow Harriers women's football team. Jess rebels against her family to join the team and finds love, friendship and a soccer scholarship at a US university.

George (**Gerard Butler**) is a former soccer star who has fallen on hard times. He tries to get his life back on track by coaching his son's football team – and so regains the boy's respect. Along the way he has to deal with his failed marriage and the attentions of amorous soccer moms.

PLAYING FOR KEEPS
2012 (USA)
$30,963,272

THE DAMNED UNITED
2009 (UK)
$4,091,378

Brian Clough (**Michael Sheen**) lives out his ill-fated 44-day managerial reign at Leeds United, as he tries to fill the impossible boots of his great rival Don Revie (**Colm Meaney**). Clough also struggles with the absence of his friend and former right-hand man Peter Taylor (**Timothy Spall**).

ESCAPE TO VICTORY
1981 (USA)
$27,453,418

Perhaps the best-loved of all football films – improbably directed by the great John Huston. In a Second World War POW camp, a group of footballing Allied prisoners, including Captain John Colby (**Michael Caine**), Captain Robert Hatch (**Sylvester Stallone**), Corporal Luis Fernandez (**Pelé**), Terry Brady (**Bobby Moore**) and Carlos Rey (**Osvaldo Ardiles**) – plus most of the early 80s Ipswich Town team – are challenged to a game in Paris against a crack German team. The film is known simply as *Victory* in the USA.

Viola Hastings (**Amanda Bynes**) loves football, but her soccer team is scrapped. So she disguises herself as her twin brother, Sebastian, goes to his school and joins the boys' team. Much romantic confusion ensues in this sporty retelling of William Shakespeare's *Twelfth Night*.

SHE'S THE MAN
2006 (USA)
$57,194,667

KICKING & SCREAMING
2005 (USA)
$56,070,433

Phil Weston (**Will Ferrell**) is a sporting failure. So is his 10-year-old son, Sam, who can't get into the soccer team coached by Phil's father, Buck (**Robert Duvall**), whose competitiveness casts a shadow of underachievement over the family. With the help of an expert neighbour, though, Phil coaches the Tigers soccer team (and his son) to success – against Buck's team.

Mexican half-brothers and banana-plantation workers Beto (**Diego Luna**) and Tato (**Gael García Bernal**) are also talented footballers, as goalkeeper and striker, respectively. A soccer scout sees them and recruits the pair for different teams in Mexico City. Fortunes rise and fall as Beto and Tato try to make a success of football against a backdrop of womanizing, singing and gambling.

GOAL!
THE DREAM BEGINS
2005 (USA)
$27,610,873

RUDO Y CURSI
2008 (Mexico)
$11,169,232

Young Mexican Santiago Muñez (**Kuno Becker**) dreams of becoming a professional footballer, but there are few chances of this while he works for his father in Los Angeles. Then, Santiago is discovered by a British football scout, who takes him to England and Newcastle United, where the dream comes true as he meets **Alan Shearer, David Beckham, Zinedine Zidane** and others – all playing themselves.

IS IT WORTH IT?

It can be an expensive business supporting a football club right through a season. So, when it comes to entertainment – particularly seeing your team score – is it good value? Take a look as this selection of European highflyers and what it cost to watch each league home goal in the 2014–15 season, based on the cheapest season ticket – and then decide who's paying through the nose or getting a bargain.

BAYERN MUNICH
£2.38
per goal over
17 home games

ARSENAL
£24.73
per goal over 19 home games

BENFICA
£1.47
per goal over 17 home games

PARIS SAINT-GERMAIN
£7.83
per goal over 17 home games

BAYER 04 LEVERKUSEN
£2.44
per goal over 17 home games

BARCELONA
£1.62
per goal over 19 home games

MANCHESTER UNITED
£12.98
per goal over 19 home games

CHELSEA
£20.83
per goal over 19 home games

REAL MADRID
£2.69
per goal over 19 home games

CELTIC
£5.86
per goal over 19 home games

AC MILAN
£5.42
per goal over 19 home games

MANCHESTER CITY
£6.80
per goal over 19 home games

MALMO
£4.66
per goal over 15 home games

PSV EINDHOVEN
£3.95
per goal over 17 home games

LIVERPOOL
£23.67
per goal over 19 home games

LIGUE 1 ... BY THE NUMBERS

Professional football came to France in 1932 with the creation of Ligue 1, won in its first season by Olympique Lillois, one of more than 70 clubs that have featured in the competition. Now, as then, 20 teams each play 38 games over the course of a season, in front of crowds that average more than 20,000.

78,056
Highest attendance, Lille v Olympique Lyonnais 2009, Stade de France

1
Monaco – the one club outside of France that plays in Ligue 1

7
Consecutive titles won by Olympique Lyonnais, 2001–08

44
Record number of goals scored in one season by Josip Skoblar for Olympique de Marseille, 1970–71

299
Goals scored in Ligue 1 by Delio Onnis, 1971–86 – the record

209

19
Clubs that have won Ligue 1:
Saint-Étienne **10**
Olympique de Marseille **9**
Nantes **8**
Monaco **7**
Olympique Lyonnais **7**
Stade de Reims **6**
Bordeaux **6**
Paris Saint-Germain **6**
Nice **4**
Lille **3**
Sète 34 **2**
Sochaux-Montbéliard **2**
Olympique Lillois **1**
RCF Paris **1**
Roubaix-Tourcoing **1**
Strasbourg **1**
Auxerre **1**
Lens **1**
Montpellier **1**

1
Ligue 1 winner of the European Cup/ Champions League – Olympique de Marseille, 1993

92
Matches that Nantes remained unbeaten at home, June 1976 to April 1981

15 YEARS 10 MONTHS 3 DAYS
Age of youngest Ligue 1 player, Laurent Paganelli of Saint-Étienne, 1978

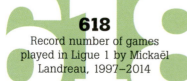

618
Record number of games played in Ligue 1 by Mickaël Landreau, 1997–2014

894
Number of games managed by Guy Roux – Auxerre 1961–2005, Lens 2007

96
Highest points in a season – Paris Saint-Germain, 2015–16

REST OF EUROPE … BY THE NUMBERS

Beyond the big five – Premier League, Bundesliga, La Liga, Serie A and Ligue 1– are nearly 50 other European leagues, stretching from Wales to Albania. They are all just as important to their local fans, and have produced some of the world's great players and managers.

14
Record number of consecutive titles won by Skonto FC in the Latvian top division, 1991–2004

28
Number of times Aris Limassol have bounced between the first and second divisions of the Cyprus league

103
Record points amassed by Celtic in the Scottish championship in the 2001–02 season

29
Consecutive wins by Benfica (Portugal), 1971–73 – a European record

1,390
Minutes that Belgian goalkeeper Dany Verlinden went without conceding a league goal for Club Brugge, March–September 1990

2016
Year that Kosovo, with its 12-team 'superleague', became the newest member of UEFA

66
Goals scored by Ferenc Déak for Szentlőrinc in the Hungarian league in one 34-game season (1945–46)

54
Scottish championships won by Rangers – a record for any European club

5
Number of teams that have won the Turkish Süper Lig:
Galatasaray 20
Fenerbahçe 19
Beşiktaş 14
Trabzonspor 6
Bursaspor 1

25
Record number of Dutch Eredivisie championships won by Ajax, with PSV Eindhoven winning 19

13
Number of times the European Cup/ Champions League has been won by a team outside the big five leagues:
Netherlands 6
Ajax 4, Feyenoord 1, PSV Eindhoven 1
Portugal 4
Benfica 2, FC Porto 2
Scotland 1
Celtic
Romania 1
Steaua Bucureşti
Yugoslavia 1
Red Star Belgrade

518
Record number of league goals scored by the Czech-Austrian Josef Bican, mostly for Slavia Prague in the Czech league, 1931–55. He is believed to have scored more than 800 goals in total

104*
Games Steaua Bucureşti went unbeaten in the Romanian top division from August 1986 to September 1989 – the European record
*some claim 106

IT'S A BALL GAME

Football – the clue is in the name. It's the single most important piece of equipment in the game, and each World Cup has had a different 'official' ball. Since 1970, all the balls have been made by Adidas, the German sports giant.

1930
URUGUAY
T-Model
Made in Britain, the ball was named for its T-shaped panel design

1934
ITALY
Federale 102
An Italian-made ball with 13 leather panels – its soft cotton laces made heading more comfortable

1938
FRANCE
Allen
The Allen, manufactured in Paris, was another 13-panel ball held together with laces

1950
BRAZIL
Super Duplo T
Made in Brazil, the first World Cup ball that could be pumped up using a hidden valve – no more laces

1954
SWITZERLAND
Swiss World Champion
Swiss-made, the ball had distinctive zigzag panels and a lighter colour for improved visibility

1958
SWEDEN
Top Star
Made by a Swedish company that won a FIFA competition, the ball had the innovation of a waxed waterproof coating

1962
CHILE
Crack
The Chile-made ball had 18 irregular polygonal panels and a new latex inflation valve

1966
ENGLAND
Slazenger Challenge 4-Star
English-made, the ball had 18 panels and came in white and yellow as well as the famous orange colour

1970
MEXICO
Telstar
The first of many World Cup balls to be made by Adidas – black and white panels helped the ball's visibility on television (hence Telstar)

1974
GERMANY
Telstar
The ball was unchanged from 1970, except for black lettering and a tougher polyurethane coating

1978
ARGENTINA
Tango
With a design that would last for the next 20 years, the ball was also the start of Adidas's tradition of choosing a name linked to the host country

1982
SPAIN
Tango España
The last genuine leather World Cup ball, with an improved plastic coating and rubber-sealed seams to aid water-resistance

1986
MEXICO
Azteca
The first ball to include designs (here, Aztec symbols) reflecting the host nation – also the first synthetic, rain-resistant ball

1990
ITALY
Etrusco
The ball decoration played on Italy's ancient past, while ball construction added a toughening layer of latex

1994
USA
Questra
US space exploration inspired the motifs on a ball that contained a layer of polystyrene foam to give it greater air speed

1998
FRANCE
Tricolore
The last of the Tango design, but the first ball to use multiple colours – influenced by the French flag, cockerel and other Gallic symbols

2002
JAPAN & S. KOREA
Fevernova
A foam layer full of tiny gas-filled balloons was one of many innovations to make this ball fly more evenly – many thought it too light

2006
GERMANY
Teamgeist
A new 14-panel design included heat-sealed rather than sewn seams – the first totally waterproof World Cup ball

2010
SOUTH AFRICA
Jabulani
Billed as the roundest and most aerodynamic ball yet, the Jabulani, meaning 'to celebrate' in Zulu, was criticized by some for its unpredictable flight

2014
BRAZIL
Brazuca
Sporting a mere six panels, the Brazuca had longer and deeper seams than other balls to help it travel further and with greater accuracy

WHO LET THE DOGS OUT?

Pitch invasions by supporters are nothing new – but those fans are usually … human. Occasionally, a non-ticket-holding member of the animal kingdom makes an entrance in a game and stops proceedings. Everything from a cow to a cat has put in an appearance, sometimes with painful consequences.

BEES
Mexico v El Salvador

A World Cup qualifier in 2009 comes to a halt when a swarm of bees invades a goalmouth.

PIGEON
Chelsea v Ipswich

During the warm-up for an FA Cup tie in 2009, a pigeon feels the full force of a Michael Ballack thunderbolt shot – and miraculously survives.

DOG
England v Brazil

In the 1962 World Cup quarterfinal in Chile, a dog runs onto the pitch, is picked up by Jimmy Greaves and urinates down the England striker's shirt. The Brazilian star Garrincha later adopts the dog.

CAT
Heracles Almelo v FC Groningen

In 2013, a black cat holds up a game in the Eredivisie – unluckily for home team Heracles, who lose 2–0.

SQUIRREL
Arsenal v Villarreal

A speedy squirrel interrupts a Champions League semifinal in 2006 to cries of 'There's only one squirrel'. It missed the return leg.

OWL
Junior Barranquilla v Deportivo Pereira

The home team's 'lucky' owl is hit by the ball during a Colombian league game in 2011. The dazed bird is then kicked by Deportivo's Luis Moreno, who needs a police escort from the ground.

COW
Polish amateur league, 2012

A confused cow enters the game, hoofs a few balls, milks the applause and heads off for an early bath.

DUCK
Zulte Waregem v Lokeren

A duck waddles into play and holds up a Belgian league game in 2010. Zulte striker Mahamadou Habib Habibou grabs the little quacker and unceremoniously lobs it over an advertising hoarding, to the resounding boos of the crowd.

The football pitch has proved fertile territory for brothers to play out their sibling rivalries or share their genetic brilliance. Chips off the same block, opposite ends of the skill spectrum, fierce rivals or inseparable team-mates – some amazing family pairings have graced the game.

ERWIN+ RONALD

ERWIN & RONALD KOEMAN
Like father, like sons – footballer Martin Koeman played for the Netherlands and so did his boys, Erwin and Ronald, who won more than 100 caps between them. Now they are together again, as coach and manager of Everton.

FRITZ+ OTTMAR

FRITZ & OTTMAR WALTER
Although Fritz was lauded as the player who pulled the strings of the West German team that defeated Hungary in the 1954 World Cup final, younger Ottmar was there, too, and outscored his brother 4–3 during the tournament. Together, they also chalked up more than 350 league games for Kaiserslautern.

FRANCO+ GIUSEPPE

FRANCO & GIUSEPPE BARESI
A giant of Italian football, Franco played more than 500 league games for AC Milan, winning 6 Serie A titles. The elder Giuseppe, also a defender, spent most of his career at Internazionale, causing serious tests of brotherly love during Milan derby matches,

MICHAEL +BRIAN

MICHAEL & BRIAN LAUDRUP
The Laudrups were arguably the most talented – and best-looking – brothers of all. Michael was the silky, penetrative midfielder with the killer pass, Brian the mesmerizing winger, their styles perfectly matched in a Denmark team that took Brazil to the wire in the World Cup quarterfinal in 1998, before losing 3–2. Michael had the more successful club career, winning 7 league titles with Juventus, Barcelona, Real Madrid and Ajax,

EDEN & THORGAN HAZARD

Football is in the Hazard boys' blood – dad played semi-professionally, and mum only gave up when pregnant with Eden, the eldest and star player for Chelsea and Belgium. Thorgan plays as an attacking midfielder for Borussia Mönchengladbach – and a third brother, Kylian, has made his mark in Hungary.

YAYA & KOLO TOURÉ

One is a steamroller of a midfielder, the other a defender who, by his own admission, is afraid of animals. Yaya and Kolo – the junior – played together for three years at Manchester City, and both have been loyal servants to the Ivory Coast national team.

SÓCRATES & RAÍ

Like his Greek philosopher namesake, Sócrates was a thinker – a journalist and doctor as well as polished midfielder. Rai played more than 200 league games for São Paulo and Paris Saint-Germain, and won the World Cup with Brazil in 1994 – something big brother never did.

JACK & BOBBY CHARLTON

Bobby's majestic goalscoring may be better remembered than Jackie's tackling, but both were key members of England's 1966 World Cup-winning team. Jackie fared better than his brother as a manager, taking the Republic of Ireland to the 1994 World Cup.

GARY & PHIL NEVILLE

The golden 'class of '92' at Manchester United included the likes of eye-catchers Beckham and Giggs, but also this ever-reliable pair, who jointly notched up 663 Premier League games for United and 144 caps for England.

XABI & MIKEL ALONSO

At one point, the Basque-born siblings were both in England – Xabi at Liverpool and Mikel at Bolton Wanderers. Now Xabi is a World Cup-winning stalwart at Bayern Munich, while big brother Mikel plies his trade in the Spanish third division.

WHISTLE BLOWERS

If you watch the game, it pays to know what the match officials – referees and their assistants – are signalling with their arms, flag and whistle. If you play the game, then it's really rather essential. Here is a quick guide to what all that waving, pointing and blowing means.

YELLOW CARD

RED CARD – SENT OFF

GOAL

DISALLOWED GOAL

PUSHING

CORNER KICK/ GOAL KICK

HAND BALL

PENALTY KICK

DIRECT FREE KICK

OBSTRUCTION

TRIPPING

KICKING

ELBOWING

PLAY ON

INDIRECT
FREE KICK

OFFSIDE/FOUL
(Assistant referee)

SUBSTITUTION
(Assistant referee)

OFFSIDE
LOCATION
(Assistant referee)

THE HANDS OF GOD

Didn't touch it, ref! It's amazing what a footballer can get away with, especially when the temptation of using their hand, rather than boot or head, takes over. Some crucial matches, including World Cup clashes, have turned on an outstretched arm unseen by the officials. 'Divine' intervention – or bare-faced cheek?

TORSTEN FRINGS

Germany 1–0 USA
2002 World Cup quarterfinal
With Germany 1–0 up, against the run of play, Torsten Frings handles the ball on the line to keep out a goal-bound shot from USA defender Gregg Berhalter. The referee and linesman don't spot it and Germany win the game.

LUIS SUÁREZ

Uruguay 1–1 Ghana
2010 World Cup quarterfinal
It's that man again. With the teams locked at 1–1, deep into extra time, Ghana player Dominic Adiyiah spears a header towards the net only for Suárez to palm the ball away. He is sent off, but Asamoah Gyan misses the penalty, Uruguay win the shoot-out 4–2 and Ghana lose the chance to become the first African nation to reach a World Cup semifinal.

LIONEL MESSI

Barcelona 2–2 Espanyol
2007 La Liga
Messi has scored many great – legal – goals, but in the season's penultimate match, with La Liga in the balance and Barcelona 1–0 down, the pocket genius punched rather than headed a cross into the net. He got away with it, the goal stood, but to no avail, as Barcelona could only draw, leaving Real Madrid to take the title.

THIERRY HENRY

France 1–1 Republic of Ireland

2009 World Cup qualifier play-off

Ireland has been off the list as a holiday destination for Thierry Henry since the night in the Stade de France when the striker handled the ball – twice – before putting William Gallas in for the goal that gave France a 2–1 aggregate victory.

JOE JORDAN

Scotland 2–0 Wales

1978 World Cup qualifier

With the score at 0–0 in a tight match, Scottish striker Jordan rises to meet a cross – which he sends on its way with a raised fist. Cruelly, a Welsh defender is pulled up for a foul, while Jordan kisses his clenched hand. Scotland score the bogus penalty, then another goal to seal Wales' fate.

DIEGO MARADONA

Argentina 2-1 England

1986 World Cup quarterfinal

And the granddaddy of them all … It's 51 minutes into the game at Mexico's Azteca Stadium. As the ball loops into England's penalty box, Maradona leaps as if to head the ball but instead punches it into the net, past Peter Shilton. The England players and more than 100,000 spectators saw it – but not the ref. Maradona later described his infamous action as the 'hand of God' and 'revenge' for his country's defeat in the Falklands War.

And one who didn't get away with murder …

PAUL SCHOLES

Manchester United 1–2 Zenit St Petersburg

2008 Champions League

In the closing minutes, with United facing defeat, Scholes has a rush of blood to the head, or rather fist, as he punches the ball – expertly – from the edge of the box into the top-left corner. He gets a second yellow card, is sent off and earns a suspension – not so clever …

TWITTERATI

For today's footballers, the roar of the crowd just isn't enough. They want to reach their fans – and be adored by them – 24/7. And what better way to keep in touch with your worshippers than a little tweeting? It's a minute-by-minute business, so, when you read this, the faces but not their numbers will be the same.

£350,000

The money the English Football Association made in 2011–14 from fining players and officials for Twitter abuse. Ashley Cole paid the highest price (£90,000) for insulting the FA itself

RONALDO
OUT-TWEETED

He may have more followers than any other sportsperson, but Cristiano doesn't make Twitter's top 10, with Katy Perry, Justin Bieber, Taylor Swift and Barack Obama in the top 4 slots

1,700,000
NUMBER OF TWEETS

generated in less than two hours by the draw for the 2014 World Cup

KAKÁ

First footballer to have

10,000,000

Twitter followers

TEAMS WITH THE MOST FOLLOWERS

1 **Real Madrid 22.3**
2 **Barcelona 20.1**
3 **Manchester United 10.3**
4 **Arsenal 9.3**
5 **Chelsea 8.1**
6 **Liverpool 6.92**
7 **Galatasaray 6.9**
8 **Al-Hilal 5.8**
9 **Fenerbahçe 5.6**
10 **Corinthians 4.9**

(in millions – February 2017 figures, twitter.com)

#Twitter Dream Team

Millions monitor their every move – the ultimate twittering line-up

(followers in millions – February 2017 figures, twitter.com)

Sergio Agüero
11.1

Neymar
27.2

Cristiano Ronaldo
50

Andrés Iniesta
15

Wayne Rooney
14.4

Mesut Özil
14.3

Gerard Piqué
13.9

David Luiz
8.3

Dani Alves
7.7

Sergio Ramos
9.4

David de Gea
6.7

And on the bench ...
Victor Valdés 4.6
Vincent Kompany 2.7
Cesc Fàbregas 9
Robin van Persie 8.6
Luis Suárez 8.6

But where's Messi?
Too modest, at a mere 1.1

GET THE TRAINER ON!

Football is not, by and large, a dangerous occupation. It does, though, have a higher incidence of injury than most other popular sports. Feet and legs, of course, take a lot of punishment, but what are the most likely injuries to bring the trainer or medics dashing onto the pitch?

12–35
Average number of injuries that happen per 1,000 hours played

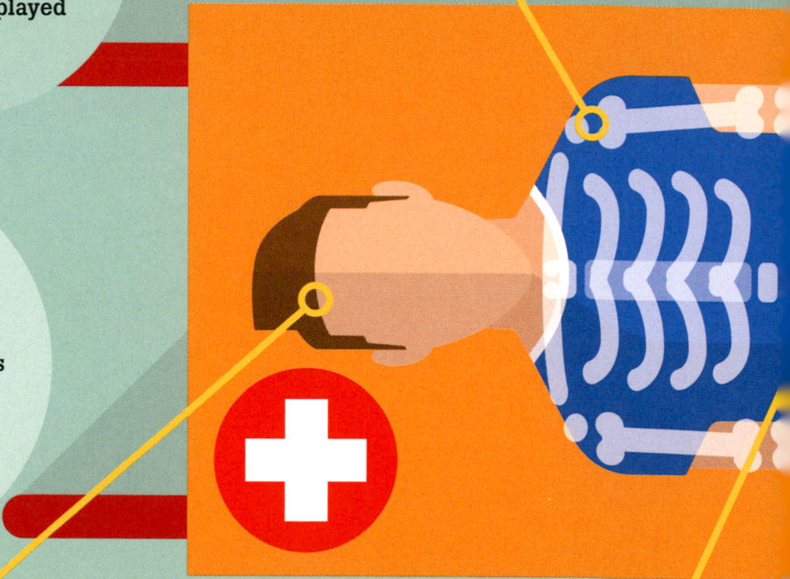

75 %
Average amount of injuries that happen to a footballer's lower extremities, from the groin and pelvis downwards

25–33 %
Average amount of football injuries that develop gradually due to overuse of a part of the body

THIGH STRAIN
upper front of leg

DISLOCATED SHOULDER

CONCUSSION

HERNIA
abdomen

HAMSTRING STRAIN
upper back of leg

KNEE CARTILAGE TEAR

CALF STRAIN

49 %

Average amount of career-ending impact injuries that involve the knee

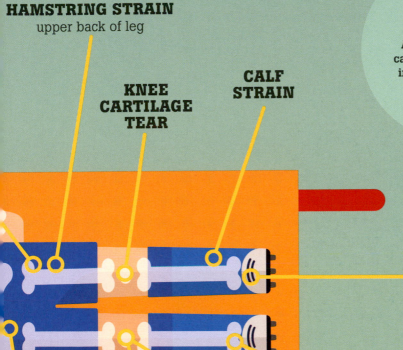

BROKEN METATARSAL
top of foot

SPRAINED ANKLE

GROIN STRAIN

ANTERIOR CRUCIATE LIGAMENT (ACL) **DAMAGE**
front of knee

MEDIAL COLLATERAL LIGAMENT (MCL) **DAMAGE**
inside/back of knee

MATTHEWS TO MESSI –
PLAYERS OF THE YEAR

Football, like all sports, loves a nice shiny awards ceremony where a player of the moment, voted the best, receives a nice shiny trophy. Surprisingly, perhaps, the world's top footballer has been crowned only since 1991. Europe started somewhat earlier in 1956 by introducing the Ballon d'Or, with Stanley Matthews, the legendary English winger, kicking things off.

BALLON D'OR

France Football magazine launched the annual award for best footballer in Europe, with the player chosen by a panel of sports journalists. At first, only a European at a European club could be chosen, but in 1995 the scope widened to include non-Europeans playing in Europe, and then extended to any world player in 2007. The Ballon d'Or merged with the FIFA World Player of the Year in 2010, but in 2016 *France Football* revived it as an independent award.

Year	Player	Country		Year	Player	Country
1956	Stanley Matthews	ENG		1983	Michel Platini	FRA
1957	Alfredo Di Stéfano	ESP		1984	Michel Platini	FRA
1958	Raymond Kopa	FRA		1985	Michel Platini	FRA
1959	Alfredo Di Stéfano	ESP		1986	Igor Belanov	URS
1960	Luis Suárez	ESP		1987	Ruud Gullit	NED
1961	Omar Sívori	ITA		1988	Marco van Basten	NED
1962	Josef Masopust	TCH		1989	Marco van Basten	NED
1963	Lev Yashin	URS		1990	Lothar Matthäus	GER
1964	Denis Law	SCO		1991	Jean-Pierre Papin	FRA
1965	Eusébio	POR		1992	Marco van Basten	NED
1966	Bobby Charlton	ENG		1993	Roberto Baggio	ITA
1967	Flórián Albert	HUN		1994	Hristo Stoichkov	BUL
1968	George Best	NIR		1995	George Weah	LIB
1969	Gianni Rivera	ITA		1996	Matthias Sammer	GER
1970	Gerd Müller	FRG		1997	Ronaldo	BRA
1971	Johan Cruyff	NED		1998	Zinedine Zidane	FRA
1972	Franz Beckenbauer	FRG		1999	Rivaldo	BRA
1973	Johan Cruyff	NED		2000	Luís Figo	POR
1974	Johan Cruyff	NED		2001	Michael Owen	ENG
1975	Oleh Blokhin	URS		2002	Ronaldo	BRA
1976	Franz Beckenbauer	FRG		2003	Pavel Nedvěd	CZE
1977	Allan Simonsen	DEN		2004	Andriy Shevchenko	UKR
1978	Kevin Keegan	ENG		2005	Ronaldinho	BRA
1979	Kevin Keegan	ENG		2006	Fabio Cannavaro	ITA
1980	Karl-Heinz Rummenigge	FRG		2007	Kaká	BRA
1981	Karl-Heinz Rummenigge	FRG		2008	Cristiano Ronaldo	POR
1982	Paolo Rossi	ITA		2009	Lionel Messi	ARG
				2016	Cristiano Ronaldo	POR

FIFA BALLON D'OR

In 2010, the FIFA world competition merged with the Ballon d'Or to create a new prize to mark the best footballer on the planet. FIFA and experts from *France Football* magazine agreed on a shortlist of players, who then received the votes of national coaches, national captains and journalists.

2010	Lionel Messi	ARG
2011	Lionel Messi	ARG
2012	Lionel Messi	ARG
2013	Cristiano Ronaldo	POR
2014	Cristiano Ronaldo	POR
2015	Lionel Messi	ARG

FIFA WORLD PLAYER OF THE YEAR

Late into the awards game, FIFA drew up a shortlist of players, with international team managers then voting for the world's best.

1991	Lothar Matthäus	GER
1992	Marco van Basten	NED
1993	Roberto Baggio	ITA
1994	Romário	BRA
1995	George Weah	LIB
1996	Ronaldo	BRA
1997	Ronaldo	BRA
1998	Zinedine Zidane	FRA
1999	Rivaldo	BRA
2000	Zinedine Zidane	FRA
2001	Luis Figo	POR
2002	Ronaldo	BRA
2003	Zinedine Zidane	FRA
2004	Ronaldinho	BRA
2005	Ronaldinho	BRA
2006	Fabio Cannavaro	ITA
2007	Kaká	BRA
2008	Cristiano Ronaldo	POR
2009	Lionel Messi	ARG

UEFA BEST PLAYER IN EUROPE

When the Ballon d'Or linked with FIFA and went worldwide in 2010, the European football governing body, UEFA, got in on the act and created its own European gong. Following the lead of the Ballon d'Or, journalists decide who receives the award, which is handed out each August.

2010–11	Lionel Messi	ARG
2011–12	Andrés Iniesta	ESP
2012–13	Franck Ribéry	FRA
2013–14	Cristiano Ronaldo	POR
2014–15	Lionel Messi	ARG
2015–16	Cristiano Ronaldo	POR

THE BEST FIFA MEN'S PLAYER

The award goalposts moved yet again in 2016, when FIFA parted company with the Ballon d'Or and *France Football* to create a new set of global football prizes, including one for the best male player. Media representatives, national team coaches, national team captains and, for the first time, football fans select the world's best.

2016	Cristiano Ronaldo	POR

PITCH PERFECT

All you need for a game of football are players, goalposts, a ball and a pitch – simple. In the professional game, however, there are strict rules and guidelines that govern the playing surface, its dimensions, markings and fixtures. FIFA lays down the law, and every team and country must follow.

Out of play

Still in play

IN PLAY – OR OUT

To be out of play a ball must completely cross the touchline or goal line, whether on the ground or in the air. If any part of the ball is on or above the line, the ball is still in play.

❶ GOALPOSTS

Goalposts and crossbars must be white and made of wood, metal or other approved material. They can be round, square, rectangular or elliptical in shape.

❷ GOAL SIZE

A goal, consisting of two vertical bars – equidistant from the corner flags – and a horizontal crossbar, must be placed in the centre of each goal line. The inner edges of the posts are 7.32m (8yd) apart, and the distance from the lower edge of the crossbar to the pitch is 2.44m (8ft).

❸ GOAL AREA

The goal area (the '6-yard box') is formed by the goal line, two lines at right angles to the goal line – 5.5m (6yd) from the inside of each goalpost and extending the same distance onto the pitch – and a line linking the two extended lines.

PLAYING SURFACE

Grass is the normal surface for a pitch, although the game can be played on natural or artificial surfaces. The colour of an artificial surface must be green.

❹ CENTRE CIRCLE

The centre point of the pitch, where the ball is placed for kick-offs, is marked at the midpoint of the halfway line. Around this, a circle (the centre circle) is marked with a radius of 9.15m (10yd). This circle indicates the minimum distance that opposing players must keep at kick-off.

❺ PITCH LENGTH

The pitch must be longer than it is wide. Both touchlines should be of an equal length, between 90m (100yd) and 120m (130yd). For international matches, the length must be between 100m (110yd) and 110m (120yd).

TOUCHLINE (full length of pitch)

ALL OF A SIZE?

Many club and international pitches now measure a standard 105m (114yd) by 68m (74yd) – but not all. Tottenham Hotspur's White Hart Lane pitch, for example, is a tighter squeeze at 100m (109yd) by 67m (73yd).

PITCH MARKINGS

The pitch must be rectangular and marked with lines no more than 12cm (5in) wide to show the relevant boundaries and areas of play. The longest boundaries are the two touchlines, and the two shorter boundaries are the goal lines. A halfway line, linking the midpoints of the touchlines, divides the pitch into two halves.

❻ PENALTY SPOT

The penalty 'mark' is 11m (12yd) in front of the midpoint between the goalposts and equidistant from each post. When a penalty kick is taken, all players, other than the penalty taker and the defending goalkeeper, must be at least 9.15m (10yd) behind the mark – a distance indicated by the penalty arc.

❼ PENALTY ARC

The arc of a circle with a radius of 9.15m (10yd), measured from the penalty mark, is drawn from the outside edge of the penalty area. This is sometimes simply called 'the D'.

❽ PITCH WIDTH

The goal lines must be of the same length, between 45m (50yd) and 90m (100yd), or between 64m (70yd) and 75m (80yd) for international matches.

❾ PENALTY AREA

The penalty area ('the 18-yard box' or just 'the box') consists of the goal line, two lines at right angles to the goal line – 16.5m (18yd) from the inside of each goalpost and extending the same distance onto the pitch – and a line linking the two extended lines.

❿ CORNERS

Each corner of the pitch must be marked by a flag and post not less than 1.5m (5ft) high. A quarter circle with a radius of 1m (1yd) is drawn inside the pitch to mark it. For a corner kick, the ball must be placed inside the arc nearest to where the ball crossed the goal line.

GOAL LINE (full width of pitch)

153

ANATOMY OF A DIVA

He's been a striker for top clubs such as Ajax, AC Milan, Barcelona, Paris Saint-Germain and Manchester United, and for Sweden. Zlatan Ibrahimović also thinks highly of himself and, as these reported quotes suggest, is not afraid of a little self-promotion or controversy.

ONE THING IS FOR SURE, A WORLD CUP WITHOUT ME IS NOTHING TO WATCH/
After Sweden's failure to qualify for the 2014 World Cup

ZLATAN DOESN'T DO AUDITIONS/
A transfer deal to Arsenal breaks down after Arsène Wenger requests a trial

WHEN YOU BUY ME, YOU ARE BUYING A FERRARI/
Zlatan sums himself up

ABSOLUTELY NOT. I HAVE ORDERED A PLANE. IT IS MUCH FASTER/
After he was rumoured to be buying a Porsche

IF HE [ROONEY] STILL WANTS TO MOVE NEXT SUMMER ... I WOULD URGE HIM TO COME AND PLAY WITH ME IN PARIS. ... IF HE DID JOIN, HE WOULD HAVE TO GET USED TO THE FACT THAT ZLATAN SCORES EVEN BETTER GOALS THAN HIM/

AN INJURED ZLATAN IS A PRETTY SERIOUS THING FOR ANY TEAM

If Zlatan can't make the team, just don't bother

I LIKE FIREWORKS TOO, BUT I SET THEM OFF IN GARDENS ... I NEVER SET FIRE TO MY OWN HOUSE

Commenting on Mario Balotelli's hapless fireworks display

NOTHING. SHE ALREADY HAS ZLATAN

His thoughts on a birthday gift for his wife

WE'RE LOOKING FOR AN APARTMENT. IF WE DON'T FIND ANYTHING, THEN I'LL PROBABLY JUST BUY THE HOTEL

Zlatan's house-hunting struggle in Paris

FIRST I WENT LEFT, HE DID TOO. THEN I WENT RIGHT, AND HE DID TOO. THEN I WENT LEFT AGAIN, AND HE WENT TO BUY A HOT DOG

Joking at the inadequacies of a Liverpool defender

I CAN'T HELP BUT LAUGH AT HOW PERFECT I AM

Zlatan sees the funny side of life

CAMPEONATO BRASILEIRO ...
BY THE NUMBERS

Brazil did not have a national football league until 1959, relying instead on regional competitions. That league, known as the Brasileiro since 1989, is now one of the world's liveliest contests, with 20 clubs, such as São Paulo's Palmeiras and Corinthians and Rio's Flamengo and Fluminense, each slugging it out over 38 games from May to December.

5

Record number of titles won by manager Vanderlei Luxemburgo – Palmeiras (1993, 1994), Corinthians (1998), Cruzeiro (2003), Santos (2004)

55

Smallest crowd to have watched a Brasileiro match – Juventude 2–1 Portuguesa, December 1997

190

Goals scored by Roberto Dinamite, 1971–93 – the Brazilian record

103

Record goal tally for champions Santos in 2004

1,000

Appearances reached in 2011 by goalkeeper Rogério Ceni for São Paulo in all competitions. He has also scored more than 100 goals

12 SECONDS

Fastest red card – Zé Carlos, for elbowing, Cruzeiro v Atlético Mineiro, July 2009

155,523

Biggest ever crowd at a Brazilian league match, Flamengo v Santos, Maracanã, May 1983

17

Clubs that have won the Brasileiro:
Palmeiras **9**
Santos **8**
São Paulo **6**
Corinthians **6**
Flamengo **5**
Cruzeiro **4**
Fluminense **4**
Vasco da Gama **4**
Internacional **3**
Bahia **2**
Botafogo **2**
Grêmio **2**
Atlético Mineiro **1**
Guarani **1**
Coritiba **1**
Sport Recife **1**
Atlético Paranaense **1**

34

Goals scored by Washington Stencanela Cerqueira (or just Washington) for Atlético Paranaense in 2004 – a Brazilian record

26

Number of managers sacked in the 2013 season, an average of 1.3 per club – Coritiba alone got through four managers

14

Record number of red cards in one game – Goiás v Cruzeiro, October 1979

5

Championships won in a row by Santos, 1961–65

REST OF SOUTH AMERICA ...
BY THE NUMBERS

There may be only 10 footballing countries in South America, but this football-mad continent is full of vibrant leagues, including Argentina's Primera División, dating from 1891. These hard-fought competitions have produced many stars, such as Alexis Sánchez and Luis Suárez.

0
Number of times a side from Peru, Bolivia or Venezuela has won the Copa Libertadores, South America's major club competition. Argentinian clubs lead the way with 24 wins

44
Years it took for a team other than Peñarol or Nacional to win the Uruguayan Primera División – Defensor, in 1976

230
Record number of goals scored by Fernando Morena in the Uruguayan Primera División, 1969–85, mostly for Peñarol

15 YEARS 35 DAYS
Age of Sergio Agüero when he made his debut for Independiente in 2003 – the youngest player in the Argentine Primera División

36
Primera División titles won by River Plate, the most successful club in Argentina

4
Occasions an Argentinian side has been runner-up in the FIFA Club World Cup – Boca Juniors 2007, Estudiantes 2009, San Lorenzo 2014 and River Plate 2015. Brazilian clubs have won the trophy 4 times

94
Uruguayan Primera División titles won by Peñarol (48) and Nacional (46)

295
Goals scored by Paraguayan striker Arsenio Erico in Argentina's Primera División, playing for Independiente 1933–46

80,093
Capacity of Estadio Monumental 'U' in Lima, home of Peruvian Primera División side Club Universitario de Deportes – the largest stadium in South America

70
Seasons the Colombian clubs Atlético Nacional, Millonarios, Independiente Santa Fe and Atlético Nacional have each appeared in the Colombian Categoría Primera A league

4,338m (14,232ft)
Height above sea level of the Estadio Daniel Alcides Carrión, in Cerro de Pasco, Peru, home of the third-tier club Unión Minas – this makes it the highest football stadium in the world. Some sources put it higher, at 4,380m (14,370ft)

FIGHTING FIT

A professional footballer can cover 10km (6 miles) in an average game so has to be in peak physical condition. Outside of a Saturday match, a pro spends most of the week training – with only one day free. Here's how a typical week's exercise and diet programme might pan out with no midweek game.

SATURDAY (POST-MATCH)
☑ **Static recovery** – ice baths and putting on compression leggings to get the blood and oxygen going

SUNDAY
☑ **Active recovery** – cycling for 20 minutes at 60 per cent heart rate

MONDAY
☑ **Extended recovery** – light football session or technical work

TUESDAY
☑ **AM:** high-intensity football work – games of few players, with no goals, keeping possession, or a game of man-to-man marking

☑ **PM:** strength and power – squats, deadlifts, bench presses, pull-ups

WEDNESDAY
☑ **AM:** moderate-to-high-intensity football work – possession drills and tactical game with 11 players

☑ **PM:** strength and explosiveness training – low repetitions at high speed of exercises such as weightlifting power cleans and hurdle jumps

THURSDAY
☑ **Rest day**

FRIDAY
☑ **Low-intensity football work** – speed and reaction training, focusing on tactical preparation, such as short shuttle runs

EAT TO WIN

There's no point doing all that training and exercise without a diet plan that gets the body into the best possible shape before, during and after a gruelling 90 minutes on the pitch. For the top footballers, it's all about getting the nutritional balance right.

BEFORE THE MATCH · PREPARATION

A balanced mix of protein and carbohydrates is important at lunch and dinner. Salmon, mackerel, turkey and beef are all good protein sources. For carbs, look beyond pasta and rice to include alternatives such as amaranth seeds and quinoa and farro grains, backed up by seasonal vegetables packed with vitamins and minerals. Breakfast is a chance for players to stock up on energy for the day's match or training, so porridge, perhaps using lighter grains such as quinoa, is popular – as are eggs. Training is increasingly explosive and demanding, so players are urged to top up on protein by taking high-protein snacks, such as flapjacks and shakes – but freshly made, to avoid too much sugar and fat.

DURING THE MATCH · MAINTENANCE

Carbohydrate and caffeine gels can boost energy levels at half-time – but the body must be trained to get used to them. Fluids containing carbohydrates to help muscles recover and electrolytes to help keep the body hydrated are vital, especially if the game is played in a hot climate. Fluid intake should be tailored to each individual player.

AFTER THE MATCH · RECOVERY

Once the final whistle has blown, it's important for players' muscles to make a quick recovery. Drinks containing carbohydrates, protein and antioxidants, such as fruit and grain smoothies, are key to this process. Then, once the body has settled, but still in the dressing room, players are encouraged to eat favourite nutrient-rich foods, such as sushi or sashimi, to aid recovery. At home, players should keep a supply of healthy topping-up essentials, such as cereals, granola, yogurt and – again – good old-fashioned eggs.

THEATRES OF CLUB DREAMS

The roar, the chants, the home supporters doing their utmost to almost suck the ball into the net – nothing beats the sheer excitement of being at a football match. Impressive club stadiums abound, but here is a selection of some that have a romance, grandeur and sporting aura second to none.

← OLD TRAFFORD
MANCHESTER, ENGLAND

Capacity **75,653** First game **1910**

Named the 'Theatre of Dreams' by Bobby Charlton, Old Trafford, England's biggest club ground and home to Manchester United, was designed by the Scottish architect Archibald Leitch, who built more than 20 British football stadiums, including White Hart Lane, Ibrox and Villa Park.

CAMP NOU →
BARCELONA, SPAIN

Capacity **99,354** First game **1957**

The largest football stadium in Europe, Camp Nou, meaning 'New Ground' in Catalan, took three years to build and went three times over budget. Its biggest attendance was 120,000 for a 1986 game between Barcelona and Juventus.

← SAN SIRO
MILAN, ITALY

Capacity **80,018** First game **1926**

Fierce rivals AC Milan and Internazionale both play at the Stadio Giuseppe Meazza, commonly called San Siro, after the district in Milan in which it stands. The stadium's 11 distinctive cylindrical towers were added in 1990.

ESTADIO SANTIAGO BERNABÉU →
MADRID, SPAIN

Capacity **81,044** First game **1947**

Real Madrid's home ground was the dream of club president Santiago Bernabéu, who gave his name to the stadium. The Bernabéu has hosted four European Cup or Champions League finals and the 1982 World Cup final.

ALLIANZ ARENA →
MUNICH, GERMANY
Capacity **71,137** First game **2005**
The Allianz Arena is Bayern Munich's third home, and also hosts Bundesliga club TSV 1860 Munich. The spectacular structure is clad in 2,874 inflated panels that allow the stadium to change colour at night.

← LA BOMBONERA
BUENOS AIRES, ARGENTINA
Capacity **49,000** First game **1940**
The Estadio Alberto J. Armando, the ground of the Boca Juniors club, gets the name La Bombonera, meaning 'The Chocolate Box', for its unusual shape, with one flat stand and three steep, curved stands.

TÜRK TELEKOM ARENA →
ISTANBUL, TURKEY
Capacity **52,650** First game **2011**
The supporters of Galatasaray, aided by the acoustics of their stadium, create one of the most intimidating atmospheres in football. In March 2011, the fans' roar was measured at 131.76 decibels – a world record at the time.

← SIGNAL IDUNA PARK
DORTMUND, GERMANY
Capacity **80,667** First game **1974**
Borussia Dortmund's ground, originally known as the Westfalenstadion, is the largest in the Bundesliga. The south stand, Europe's biggest terrace, holds 25,000 fans.

CELTIC PARK →
GLASGOW, SCOTLAND
Capacity **60,832** First game **1892**
Scene of many football battles with long-time Glasgow adversaries Rangers, Celtic's old ground reached its highest attendance of 92,000 for an 'Old Firm' derby in 1938. According to no less a person than Lionel Messi, Celtic Park has 'the best atmosphere in Europe'.

FOOTBALL CRAZY

Sometimes skill just isn't enough, and even the greatest players resort to a collection of strange rituals to try to influence the result and their performance. Then there are those sensitive souls for whom the world beyond the football pitch can be a scary place.

SOCCER SUPERSTITIONS

JOHN TERRY
P FOR PARTICULAR

• The Chelsea defender always has to use the same urinal in the home dressing room.

SERGIO GOYCOCHEA
P FOR PENALTY

• Once, before facing a penalty, the Argentinian goalkeeper took a pitch-side pee – he saved the shot, so from then on he relieved himself quickly before facing any penalty.

JOHAN CRUYFF
TUM AND GUM

• Before each game at Ajax, the Dutch master would slap the goalkeeper, Gert Bals, in the stomach and spit chewing gum into the opposing team's half.

BOBBY MOORE
NO, AFTER YOU …

• England's 1966 World Cup-winning captain would never pull on his shorts before a game until all the other players had donned theirs.

KOLO TOURÉ

The Ivorian defender's ritual of always being the last man onto the pitch backfired in 2009 when, then an Arsenal player, he was booked for joining the second half of a game against AS Roma after the action had already begun.

LEV YASHIN

The great Russian goalkeeper's recipe for perfect game preparation? 'Have a smoke to calm the nerves, then toss back a drink to tone the muscles.'

LAURENT BLANC
SEALED WITH A KISS

• On the way to victory at the 1998 World Cup, the France sweeper planted a smacker on the bald head of goalkeeper Fabien Barthez before every game, including the final – even though Blanc was banned from that match.

GARY LINEKER
SETTLING THE SCORER

• The prolific England striker never took a shot in a match warm-up for fear of wasting a goal. He would also change his shirt at half-time if he had not scored and get a haircut whenever his goals dried up.

PEPE REINA
FILLING UP

• When the Spanish goalkeeper played home games for Liverpool he would take his car to the same petrol station before the match and fill the tank. The night before any game Reina would always have two cheese and ham toasties and a glass of wine.

GENNARO GATTUSO
PERFECT TOILET READING

• Before each game at the 2006 World Cup, the hard-boiled Italian midfielder displayed his more sensitive side by reading a few pages from the Russian master Dostoevsky – while on the loo. It seemed to do the trick as Italy went on to win the final.

FOOTIE PHOBIAS

DAVID BECKHAM
MR PERFECT

Ataxophobia – a fear of disorder and chaos
Becks will rearrange objects by colour – and if there happen to be three cans in the fridge, he is likely to remove one of them to ensure an even number.

SHAY GIVEN

The Stoke City and Republic of Ireland goalkeeper is said to place a vial of holy water in the back of his goal at every match.

DENNIS BERGKAMP
GROUNDED GENIUS

Aerophobia – a fear of flying
The Dutchman's phobia dates back to the amount of flying involved in getting to, from and around the 1994 World Cup in the United States. When he joined Arsenal in 1995, Bergkamp refused to fly and missed many European away fixtures.

WAYNE ROONEY
LONELY BOY

Monophobia – an acute fear of being alone
When in a hotel room, Wayne sleeps with the lights, TV and even hairdryer switched on.

PHIL JONES
I'LL TAKE THE STAIRS

A fear of – foreign – lifts
The Manchester United and England defender cannot use a lift if the team are playing abroad. Apparently, he got stuck in a lift as a child on a family holiday to Greece.

10

I'M A CELEBRITY – GET ME IN THERE!

Most football fans are just part of the crowd. There are some, though, who are too famous to go unnoticed. Actors, writers, musicians, sports stars, politicians, even reigning monarchs – their club allegiances pack a few surprises.

REAL MADRID
Robert De Niro
Juan Carlos I of Spain
Jennifer Lopez
Rafael Nadal
Plácido Domingo
Julio Iglesias
Shakira
Penelope Cruz

ASTON VILLA
David Cameron
Prince William
Ozzy Osbourne
Nigel Kennedy

MÁLAGA
Antonio Banderas
(also Real Madrid)

SWANSEA
Catherine Zeta-Jones

ELIZABETH II
ARSENAL

Fans don't come any higher. The Queen has been a 'Gooner' for more than 50 years, following the allegiance of her mother, who was drawn to the team by her admiration for the Arsenal player, and England cricketer, Denis Compton.

OTHER FANS INCLUDE:
Kevin Costner, Mick Jagger, Prince Harry, Jay-Z, Lewis Hamilton

LIVERPOOL
Dr Dre
Courtney Love
Samuel L. Jackson
Daniel Craig
Nelson Mandela
Elvis Costello
Angelina Jolie
Gary Barlow
Liam Neeson
Mike Myers

BAYERN MUNICH
Nico Rosberg
Wladimir Klitschko
Steffi Graf
Boris Becker
Pope Benedict XVI

NORWICH
Hugh Jackman
Stephen Fry
Delia Smith

MANCHESTER UNITED
Rory McIlroy
Justin Timberlake
Usain Bolt
Miley Cyrus
Rihanna
Morrissey

STURM GRAZ
Arnold Schwarzenegger

VLADIMIR PUTIN
ZENIT ST PETERSBURG

St Petersburg is the home town of the sport-loving macho Russian leader, so it's hardly surprising that Zenit St Petersburg is his team. Putin even waded into a club controversy in 2012, backing the owners over their outlay of more than £60 million on two players – Hulk of Brazil and Axel Witsel of Belgium.

BURNLEY
Prince Charles

INTERNAZIONALE
Andrea Bocelli
Valentino Rossi

SAINT-ÉTIENNE
Alain Prost

CHELSEA
Ed Sheeran
Will Ferrell
Michael Caine
Steve McQueen
Jimmy Page
Gordon Ramsay
Richard Attenborough

EVERTON
Paul McCartney
Sylvester Stallone
John Hurt
Judi Dench

MILLWALL
Daniel Day-Lewis

BARCELONA
Justin Bieber
Salvador Dalí
José Carreras
Ernest Hemingway

PARIS SAINT-GERMAIN
Nicolas Sarkozy

BARACK OBAMA
WEST HAM UNITED
On a visit to his half-sister Auma in London in 2003, Obama attended a West Ham home game. The 44th US President is said to have followed the Hammers ever since.

OTHER FANS INCLUDE:
Elijah Wood, Matt Damon, Russell Brand, Keira Knightley, Alfred Hitchcock, Ray Winstone, James Corden

NEWCASTLE UNITED
Tony Blair
Sting
Mark Knopfler

AC MILAN
Novak Djokovic
(also Red Star Belgrade)

WIGAN ATHLETIC
Mikhail Gorbachev

AUXERRE
Gérard Depardieu

GENOA
Frank Sinatra

AS ROMA
Monica Bellucci
Ennio Morricone

CORINTHIANS
Ayrton Senna

JUVENTUS
Luciano Pavarotti
Carla Bruni

RANGERS
Sean Connery

EINTRACHT FRANKFURT
Sebastian Vettel

WATFORD

Elton John

LAZIO
Will Smith

CELTIC
Rod Stewart
Bono
Bob Marley

NAPOLI
Danny DeVito
Sophia Loren

ANGELA MERKEL
BORUSSIA DORTMUND
The German Chancellor is a self-confessed football nut, cheering her nation to World Cup victory in 2014. She has a soft spot for Borussia Dortmund, but, ever the diplomat, she has expressed her admiration also for Bayern Munich.

AMERICAN DREAM

North America, Central America, the Caribbean – such different regions, but they all come together under the footballing banner of the CONCACAF governing body. And since 1963, CONCACAF has organized a tournament to find the best in the Americas, first as the Championship and then, from 1991, as the Gold Cup. Mexico and the USA have dominated proceedings for the past 25 years, though Jamaica came close to spoiling the party in 2015.

CONCACAF CHAMPIONSHIP

	HOST	WINNER	RUNNER-UP
1963	El Salvador	Costa Rica	El Salvador
1965	Guatemala	Mexico	Guatemala
1967	Honduras	Guatemala	Mexico
1969	Costa Rica	Costa Rica	Guatemala
1971	Trinidad & Tobago	Mexico	Haiti
1973	Haiti	Haiti	Trinidad & Tobago
1977	Mexico	Mexico	Haiti
1981	Honduras	Honduras	El Salvador
1985	(none fixed)	Canada	Honduras
1989	(none fixed)	Costa Rica	USA

10

Number of times Mexico has won either the Championship or the Gold Cup

CONCACAF GOLD CUP

	HOST	WINNER	RUNNER-UP
1991	USA	USA	Honduras
1993	USA/Mexico	Mexico	USA
1996	USA	Mexico	Brazil (guest)
1998	USA	Mexico	USA
2000	USA	Canada	Colombia (guest)
2002	USA	USA	Costa Rica
2003	USA/Mexico	Mexico	Brazil (guest)
2005	USA	USA	Panama
2007	USA	USA	Mexico
2009	USA	Mexico	USA
2011	USA	Mexico	USA
2013	USA	USA	Panama
2015	USA/Canada	Mexico	Jamaica

6

Number of guest nations that have played in the Gold Cup: Brazil, Colombia, Ecuador, Peru, South Africa, South Korea

7

Record number of goals scored by one player in a single Gold Cup tournament – Javier Hernández (Mexico) in 2011 and Clint Dempsey (USA) in 2015

LANDON DONOVAN
USA
Highest goalscorer
in the Gold Cup
with 18 goals

GAME OVER!

Football matches almost invariably end after 90-odd minutes when the final whistle blows. But there are freakish games where, due to man-made or heaven-sent circumstances beyond the referee's control, the action ends all too abruptly – or never starts at all.

CLOSED SHOP

Mexico's football league was disrupted by the swine flu pandemic of 2009. On one weekend, 176 matches, from the 1st, 2nd and 3rd leagues, were played behind closed doors.

REVERENCE FOR HIS REVERENCE

On Saturday 2 April 2005, Pope John Paul II died. As a mark of respect, all Serie A matches in Italy were cancelled. 'It's fair that the sport is stopped … there are more important things than soccer,' said Cagliari captain Gianfranco Zola.

NO DAVID DOWN UNDER

LA Galaxy had planned a trip to Australia in December 2008 to play a promotional match against Queensland Roars. The game and trip were cancelled, however, when it became clear that David Beckham was planning a move from Galaxy to AC Milan and was not prepared to risk his fitness.

A BIT ONE-SIDED

As the Scotland team prepared for kick-off on 9 October 1999 in the Estonian capital, Tallinn, there was one problem – no opposition. The Estonians had refused to turn up in protest at a change in the timing of the match, following a Scottish complaint about the quality of the floodlights. Within seconds, the ref blew his whistle and that was that.

BOLT FROM THE BLUE

João Contreras, 21, of Sport Águila was struck down by a lightning bolt during the second leg of a Copa Peru semifinal in December 2014 against Fuerza Minera in the Peruvian city of Huancayo. The match was swiftly abandoned, and thankfully Contreras survived.

REMOTE-CONTROLLED RUMPUS

Late in the first half of a Euro 2016 qualifier between Serbia and Albania in October 2014, played in front of Serbian fans only, a remote-controlled drone flew over the pitch, unfurling a flag carrying the insignia of 'Greater Albania'. The flag was caught by a Serbian player, which led to a melee involving players, officials and supporters. The Albanian team fled the pitch, and the English referee, Martin Atkinson, abandoned the match.

A RED MIST DESCENDS

A world record was set in 2011 when referee Damian Rubino showed a staggering 36 red cards in a match between Claypole and Victoriano Arenas in the Argentine 5th division. In the second half, with two players already sent off, the game turned into a mass brawl, involving both teams, their managers and coaching staff. By the time the fans joined in there was no one left to play the game.

THE INCREDIBLE SHRINKING SQUAD

Players from the Eritrean national team have made a habit of absconding when abroad. In 2015, 10 defected after a World Cup qualifier in Botswana. Three years earlier, 17 players and the team doctor are said to have made a break for it when in Uganda, while, in 2010, 13 squad members disappeared in Tanzania, some of them later resurfacing in Texas.

GAME ECLIPSED

On 11 August 1999, people in the United Kingdom were eagerly awaiting their first total solar eclipse since 1927. This proved too much for the Devon police, who ordered the postponement of a match between Torquay United and Portsmouth, fearing they would not have enough resources to deal with the number of incidents that might be caused by the blackout.

FOOTBALL GOES POP!

'Stick to the day job' is what footballers should be told before venturing into a recording studio, and many are the toe-curlingly terrible songs they have mumbled their way through. And yet, against all odds, some players have managed to break into the pop charts – and even take top spot.

JOHAN CRUYFF
Netherlands
Oei Oei Oei
(dat was me weer een loei)
1969

▶ **Chart 21** – Netherlands • Cruyff was so nervous during recording that he had to be plied with drink before he could sing

KEVIN KEEGAN
England
Head Over Heels In Love
1979

▲ **Chart 31** – UK; **10** – Germany; **20** – Austria • Keegan's 1980 follow-up 'England' failed to make the charts

SLAVEN BILIĆ & RAWBAU
Croatia
Vatreno Ludilo (Fiery Madness)
2008

▶ **Chart 1** – Croatia • Bilić, now manager of West Ham United, plays rhythm guitar in the rock band Rawbau

▼ **Chart 31** – UK • Gazza's duet with the band Lindisfarne in 1990 on 'Fog on the Tyne (Revisited)' amazingly reached number 2 in the UK charts

PAUL GASCOIGNE
England
Geordie Boys (Gazza Rap)
1990

▶ **Chart 31** – Germany • The Kaiser's 1967 follow-up, 'Du Bist das Glück', didn't chart and spelled the end, thankfully, of his singing career

FRANZ BECKENBAUER
Germany
Du Allein/Gute Freunde Kann Niemand Trennen
1966

▶ **Chart 12** – UK • The Tottenham Hotspur and England boys' follow-up, 'It's Goodbye', could only reach 92 in the UK chart

MORTEN GAMST PEDERSEN • THE PLAYERS
Norway
This Is For Real
2006

GLENN HODDLE & CHRIS WADDLE
England
Diamond Lights
1987

▲ **Chart 11** – Norway • Morten's boy band team-mates were fellow Norwegian footballers Freddy dos Santos, Raymond Kvisvik, Kristofer Hæstad and Øyvind Svenning

ROQUE SANTA CRUZ/SPORTFREUNDE STILLER
Paraguay
Ich, Roque
2004

ASAMOAH GYAN/CASTRO
Ghana
African Girls
2011

RUUD GULLIT
Netherlands
Not The Dancing Kind
1984

▲ **Chart 32** – Germany; **38** – Austria • At the time Roque was a star stiker at Bayern Munich

◀ **Chart 4** – Netherlands • Ruud also had a number 3 hit in the Netherlands in 1988 with an anti-apartheid song, 'South Africa'

▲ **Chart 1** – Ghana • Ghanaian rapper Castro disappeared in July 2014 while jet-skiing on holiday with Gyan's family

WHO'S IN CHARGE?

Football is a truly global game and the most popular team sport on the planet, played and watched by billions. This takes a lot of organizing, both on a world and continental level, involving men's and women's tournaments, the wider promotion of the game and the setting of its rules and regulations.

FIFA
FÉDÉRATION INTERNATIONALE DE FOOTBALL ASSOCIATION
HQ: ZURICH, SWITZERLAND

World football is controlled by FIFA, founded in Paris on 21 May 1904 by delegates from Belgium, Denmark, France, the Netherlands, Spain, Sweden and Switzerland. FIFA, with its 211 member associations, defines and defends the laws of the game and supports the development of football worldwide. Jules Rimet, who served as president from 1921 to 1954, set up the first World Cup in 1930 and moved FIFA headquarters to Zurich in 1932.

1 CONCACAF
CONFEDERATION OF NORTH, CENTRAL AMERICA AND CARIBBEAN ASSOCIATION FOOTBALL
HQ: MIAMI, USA

Formed in 1961, in Mexico City, CONCACAF has 41 member football associations, including USA, Canada and Mexico, the countries of Central America and the Carribbean and two nations – Suriname and Guyana – on the northwest South American coast. CONCACAF organizes the region's major club competition, the Champions League, and the biennial Gold Cup international tournament.

2 CONMEBOL
CONFEDERACIÓN SUDAMERICANA DE FÚTBOL
HQ: LUQUE, PARAGUAY

CONMEBOL may have the fewest associations – 10 – but these include the footballing giants of Brazil, Argentina and Uruguay, who between them have won 9 out of 20 World Cups. It is the oldest continental confederation, founded in 1916 to coincide with the centenary of Argentina's declaration of independence. Among the competitions CONMEBOL organizes are the annual Copa Libertadores (for clubs) and the Copa América, a tournament held since 1916 to find the champion South American association.

3 CAF
CONFEDERATION OF AFRICAN FOOTBALL
HQ: 6th OF OCTOBER CITY, EGYPT

Four African nations, Egypt, Sudan, Ethiopia and South Africa, came together in the Sudanese capital, Khartoum, in 1957 to found CAF, which has now grown to represent 56 member associations, making it the largest of the continental confederations. CAF-organized events include the Africa Cup of Nations, held at variable intervals since 1957, and the CAF Champions League club competition.

6 UEFA
UNION OF EUROPEAN FOOTBALL ASSOCIATIONS
HQ: NYON, SWITZERLAND

Formed in Basle, Switzerland, in 1954, UEFA embraces within its 55 member associations all of Europe's football nations, plus some, such as Israel and Kazakhstan, that are either entirely outside or only partly within Europe. UEFA is, in footballing terms, the most successful confederation, with 11 World Cup winners, and it organizes the European Championship, the Champions League and the Europa League.

PLAYER POWER

Many famous footballers make the move into team management but few venture into the sometimes murky political waters of football administration. The most signifant exception has been the French midfield genius Michel Platini, winner of the Ballon d'Or in 1983, 1984 and 1985. He is the only former professional player to have held the presidency of UEFA.

5 AFC
ASIAN FOOTBALL CONFEDERATION
HQ: KUALA LUMPUR, MALAYSIA

The most extensive confederation geographically, the AFC is also the most diverse, its 47 member associations ranging from the tiny Northern Mariana Islands (population 53,500) to the People's Republic of China (population 1.35 billion). Formed in 1954, in the Philippines' capital, Manila, the AFC organizes numerous competitions, including the Asian Champions League for clubs and the Asian Cup, held every four years to crown the top country across the confederation.

4 OFC
OCEANIA FOOTBALL CONFEDERATION
HQ: AUCKLAND, NEW ZEALAND

With only 11 full members, including New Zealand, Samoa and Fiji, and 3 associate members (Kiribati, Niue Islands and Tuvalu), OFC is the smallest confederation. Formed in 1966, OFC joined FIFA in 1996 but then lost its largest member nation, Australia, to the AFC in 2006. Every two years, the OFC countries compete in the region's main competition, the Nations Cup.

PLAYING AWAY FROM HOME

What greater honour can there be than playing for the country of your birth? Well, perhaps playing instead for a different country. Some illustrious footballers have not only turned out for an adopted nation, but even played – and, heaven forbid, scored – against the motherland.

Podolski scored two goals against Poland, his birth country, at Euro 2008

LUKAS PODOLSKI
BORN: POLAND
1985

OMAR SÍVORI
BORN: ARGENTINA
1935

DEBUT: ARGENTINA 1956 **19 caps**

DECO
BORN: BRAZIL
1977

BERND KRAUSS
BORN: GERMANY
1957

ALFREDO DI STÉFANO
BORN: ARGENTINA
1926

DEBUT: ARGENTINA 1947 **6 caps**

JOSIP ŠIMUNIĆ
BORN: AUSTRALIA
1978

DEBUT: CROATIA 2001 **105 caps**

JONATHAN DE GUZMÁN
CANADA TO NETHERLANDS

- Born 1987 in Toronto, with a Filipino father and Jamaican mother, moved to the Netherlands in 1999 and took Dutch citizenship in 2008
- First game for the Netherlands in 2013
- Brother Julian played for Canada

AS IRISH AS A RED LONDON BUS

ENGLAND TO REPUBLIC OF IRELAND

When the Republic took on England in a 1990 World Cup group match, 6 of the 11 players were English-born:

Chris Morris, Mick McCarthy, Paul McGrath, John Aldridge, Tony Cascarino, Andy Townsend

BRAZILIAN EXODUS

DIEGO COSTA to Spain
THIAGO MOTTA to Italy
CACAU to Germany
PEPE to Portugal

DEBUT: GERMANY 2004 **129 caps**

- First played against Poland in a group game at the 2006 World Cup.

DEBUT: ITALY 1961 **9 caps**

- Sívori helped Argentina to win the 1957 South American Football Championship. After joining Juventus and gaining Italian citizenship, he played against Argentina in 1961, scoring twice in a 4–1 victory.

DEBUT: PORTUGAL 2003 **75 caps**

- Deco made his debut for Portugal in a 2003 match against Brazil – he scored in a 2–1 win.

DEBUT: AUSTRIA 1981 **22 caps**

- Kraus played against West Germany in 1981, scoring an own goal in a 2–0 defeat. He also faced his mother country in a 1982 World Cup group game, with Austria losing 1–0.

DEBUT: COLOMBIA 1949 **4 caps** (not recognized by FIFA)

DEBUT: SPAIN 1957 **31 caps**

- An Argentine footballing strike in 1949 led to Di Stéfano moving to Colombia, where he was called up for the national team. He joined Real Madrid in 1953, took Spanish citizenship in 1956 and played against Argentina in 1960.

- Šimunić played against Australia in a 2006 World Cup group match that ended 2–2. He was born and raised in Australia, but with ethnically Croat parents. His final club was Dinamo Zagreb.

LOST IN TRANSLATION

When that ball hits the back of the net, then out goes the shout
– gooooooal! Or usually something very similar – but sometimes
different, depending on which language you speak. All tongues
share the exclamation mark, though the volume of delivery will
vary depending on national temperament.

GÔL!
Welsh

TOR!
German

GOLI!
Swahili

进球
(JÌN QIÚ) Mandarin

GOOOOOOOOOLLLLLLLLL
Spanish/Italian/Romanian/Bulgarian/Polish/Croatian … and many more

GOL!
Turkish

DOEL!
Dutch/Afrikaans

MARK!
Icelandic

QOL!
Azerbaijani

BÁIR!
Gaelic

LADUMA!

Zulu

ゴール

(GÔRU) Japanese

GOAL!

English

LLLLLLLLLLLLLLLLLLLLL !!!!!!!!!

GOLO!

Portuguese/Esperanto

MÅL!

Swedish/Norwegian/Danish

MAALI!

Finnish

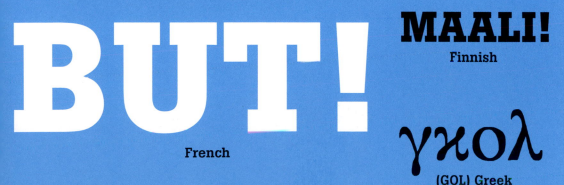

French

γχολ

(GOL) Greek

MAJOR LEAGUE SOCCER ...
BY THE NUMBERS

A new national league was part of the deal for the US to host the 1994 World Cup. The result was Major League Soccer (MLS), which has grown from 10 teams in 1996 to 22 teams – 19 in the US, 3 in Canada – divided into a Western Conference and Eastern Conference. Each team plays 34 games, with the best-performing team overall winning the Supporters' Shield, and the top 12 conference teams going on to contest the MLS Cup.

416
Record number of games played by Kevin Hartman for LA Galaxy, Kansas City Wizards and FC Dallas, 1997–2012

92,650
Highest attendance at an MLS match – Chivas USA v New England Revolution, Los Angeles Memorial Coliseum, 6 August 2006. It was a 1–1 draw

26
Record number of assists made in one season (2000) by Carlos Valderrama for Tampa Bay Mutiny

27
Record for goals scored in an MLS season – Roy Lassiter (Tampa Bay Mutiny, 1996), Chris Wondolowski (San Jose Earthquakes, 2012), Bradley Wright-Phillips (New York Red Bulls, 2014)

3
Wins for D.C. United in 2013 – lowest ever in an MLS season

11
Teams that have won the Supporters' Shield:
D.C. United **4**
LA Galaxy **4**
Columbus Crew **3**
San Jose Earthquakes **2**
New York Red Bulls **2**
Chicago Fire **1**
Sporting Kansas City **1**
Seattle Sounders **1**
Miami Fusion **1**
Tampa Bay Mutiny **1**
FC Dallas **1**

15
Longest winning streak of games – LA Galaxy, 7 September 1997 to 17 May 1998

$285 MILLION
The value in 2016 of Seattle Sounders, which makes it the most valuable MLS team

11
Teams that have won the MLS Cup:
LA Galaxy **5**
D.C. United **4**
Sporting Kansas City **2**
San Jose Earthquakes **2**
Houston Dynamo **2**
Chicago Fire **1**
Columbus Crew **1**
Real Salt Lake **1**
Colorado Rapids **1**
Portland Timbers **1**
Seattle Sounders **1**

145
Goals scored by Landon Donovan – the most prolific striker in MLS – for San Jose Earthquakes and LA Galaxy 2001–16. Donovan also has the highest assists total – 136

2

Number of MLS teams that have won the CONCACAF Champions League – D.C. United (1998), LA Galaxy (2000)

REST OF THE WORLD ...
BY THE NUMBERS

There are 211 countries with football associations affiliated to FIFA – that's a lot of national leagues, with thousands of clubs vying to be the champion in their neck of the global woods. Some, like the Japanese J1 League and Mexican Liga MX, have a huge, passionate following, others have small but diehard fan bases. Here are some intercontinental highlights.

2
Clubs that have been part of J1, the top flight of the Japanese J.League, since it kicked off in 1993 – Kashima Antlers and Yokohama F. Marinos

72,327
Capacity of the Nissan Stadium, the biggest in the J.League and home to Yokohama F. Marinos

312
Goals scored in Mexico's Liga MX by Brazilian Evanivaldo Castro (1974–88)

40 YEARS 320 DAYS
Age of Brazilian legend Romário when, playing for Adelaide United against Newcastle Jets in December 2006, he became Australian A-League's oldest player

725
Record number of Liga MX appearances by Oswaldo Sánchez (1993–2014), mostly for CD Guadalajara and Santos Laguna

8
Record number of J1 League titles won by Kashima Antlers

48
Age of striker Kazuyoshi Miura when he signed a new one-year contract with J.League 2 side Yokohama FC in November 2015. He is, unsurprisingly, the J.League's oldest scorer

1983
Year of the first season in the South Korean K League – won by the wonderfully named Hallelujah FC, a team of Christian players and coaches

6
Chinese Super League championships won by Guangzhou Evergrande. Next best is Shandong Luneng with 3 titles

11
Record number of winners of the Asian Football Confederation (AFC) Champions League that have come from South Korea. Pohang Steelers lead the field with 3 titles

58m (190ft)
Distance Fagiano Okayama FC's Ryujiro Ueda headed the ball to score from inside his own half in a 2011 J.League 2 game against Yokohama FC

HAT-TRICK HEROES

Some of the best things come in threes – and that includes goals. A trio of strikes in one game is special for any player, even Lionel Messi, who has notched up more than 30 already for Barcelona. Some hat-tricks, though, are more special than others.

90 SECONDS
Tommy Ross
Fastest ever hat-trick in professional football
Ross County 8–1 Nairn County
Scotland, November 1964

2:56
2 MINUTES 56 SECONDS
Sadio Mané
Fastest Premier League hat-trick
Southampton 6–1 Aston Villa
May 2015

18 MINUTES
Michel Platini
The 'perfect' hat-trick – left foot, header, right foot – all within 18 minutes
France 3–2 Yugoslavia
1984 European Championship

3:22

Robert Lewandowski
Bayern Munich

3 minutes, 22 seconds
BAYERN MUNICH 5–1 VFL WOLFSBURG
Bundesliga, September 2015

Fastest Bundesliga hat-trick, on the way to scoring 5 goals
• Also fastest to 4 and 5 goals in Bundesliga history
• Only Bundesliga sub to score 5

Lewandowski had, only three months earlier, in June 2015, scored a hat-trick in 4 minutes for Poland in a 4–0 defeat of Georgia in a Euro 2016 qualifying match

1
FIRST
Bert Patenaude
First hat-trick in a World Cup
USA 3–0 Paraguay
1930 World Cup

1
ONLY
Geoff Hurst
Only hat-trick in a World Cup final
England 4–2 West Germany
1966 World Cup

1
GOALKEEPER
José Luis Chilavert
Only professional goalkeeper to score a hat-trick (3 penalties)
Velez Sarsfield 6–1 Ferro Carril Oeste
Argentine league, 1999

2
TWO-IN-ONE
Two hat-tricks in one World Cup

Sándor Kocsis
Hungary 9–0 South Korea
Hungary 8–3 West Germany
1954 World Cup

Just Fontaine
France 7–3 Paraguay
France 6–3 West Germany
1958 World Cup

Gerd Müller
West Germany 5–2 Bulgaria
West Germany 3–1 Peru
1970 World Cup

3
HEADERS
Hat-trick of headers in one World Cup

Tomáš Skuhravý
Czechoslovakia 4–1 Costa Rica
Group game, 1990 World Cup

Miroslav Klose
Germany 8–0 Saudi Arabia
Group game, 2002 World Cup

2
ONE-IN-TWO
Only player to score a hat-trick in two different World Cups

Gabriel Batistuta
Argentina 4–0 Greece
21 June, 1994 World Cup
Argentina 5–0 Jamaica
21 June, 1998 World Cup

1
DEBUT
Only player to score a hat-trick on his international debut

Guillermo Stábile
Argentina 6–3 Mexico
Group game, 1930 World Cup

17 YEARS
244 DAYS
Pelé
Age when the Brazilian scored a hat-trick in a semifinal victory over France – making him the youngest player ever to score a World Cup hat-trick
Brazil 5–2 France
1958 World Cup

CLUB CAST OF HUNDREDS

Time was when one man and his dog could run a football team. Now, the top clubs are big businesses, employing – as well as a squad of players – hundreds of people to cover finance, catering, hospitality, marketing, ticketing and more. Here, based on Premier League club West Ham United, are the 200-plus people who might make up the staff.

15 CHARITY FOUNDATION

14 MATCH-DAY HOSPITALITY

17 STADIUM MANAGEMENT

22 COMMERCIAL/MARKETING/PR

23 RETAIL/TICKET SALES

11 GROUND STAFF

3 SECURITY

3 DIRECTORS

3 BOARD

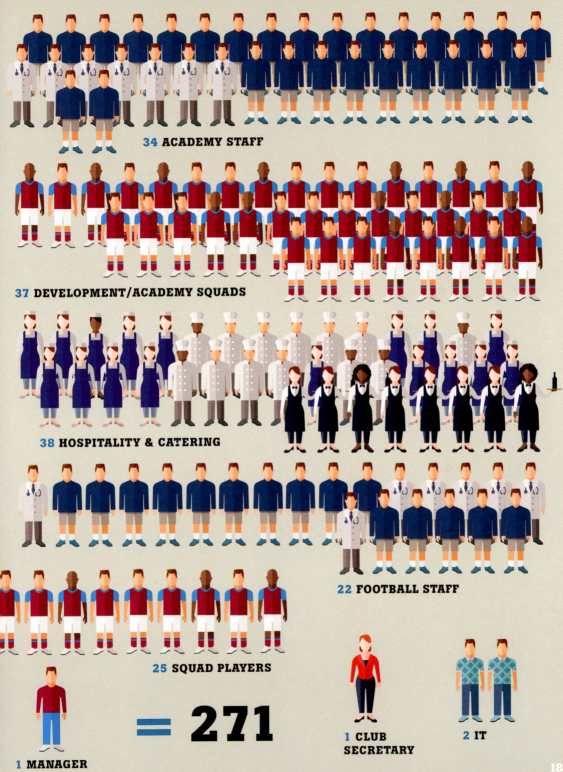

34 ACADEMY STAFF

37 DEVELOPMENT/ACADEMY SQUADS

38 HOSPITALITY & CATERING

22 FOOTBALL STAFF

25 SQUAD PLAYERS

= 271

1 MANAGER

1 CLUB SECRETARY

2 IT

A GOAL A MINUTE

Every minute counts in a football match. Only two players, though, have gone as far as scoring in each of those 90 minutes – prolific marksmen whose hunger for goals never switches off. Zlatan Ibrahimović achieved the landmark with a 24th minute goal for Sweden against Estonia in September 2014, but Cristiano Ronaldo got there first, in the 7th minute of a Real Madrid win over Atlético Madrid in February the same year. Here's a breakdown of his goals.

FIRST HALF

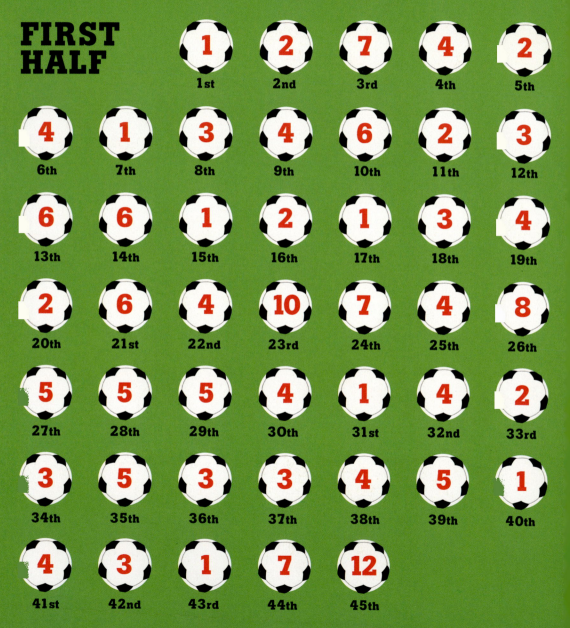

1	2	7	4	2
1st	2nd	3rd	4th	5th

4	1	3	4	6	2	3
6th	7th	8th	9th	10th	11th	12th

6	6	1	2	1	3	4
13th	14th	15th	16th	17th	18th	19th

2	6	4	10	7	4	8
20th	21st	22nd	23rd	24th	25th	26th

5	5	5	4	1	4	2
27th	28th	29th	30th	31st	32nd	33rd

3	5	3	3	4	5	1
34th	35th	36th	37th	38th	39th	40th

4	3	1	7	12
41st	42nd	43rd	44th	45th

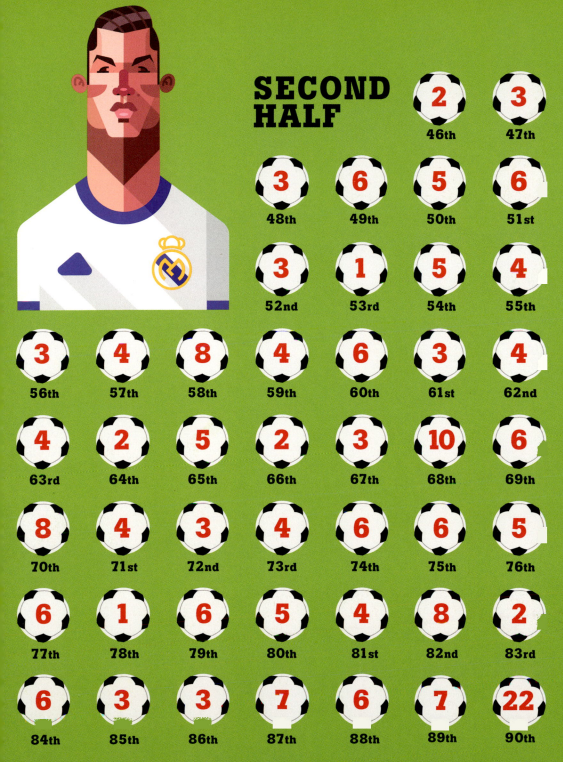

SECOND HALF

2 46th	**3** 47th

3 48th	**6** 49th	**5** 50th	**6** 51st
3 52nd	**1** 53rd	**5** 54th	**4** 55th

3 56th	**4** 57th	**8** 58th	**4** 59th	**6** 60th	**3** 61st	**4** 62nd
4 63rd	**2** 64th	**5** 65th	**2** 66th	**3** 67th	**10** 68th	**6** 69th
8 70th	**4** 71st	**3** 72nd	**4** 73rd	**6** 74th	**6** 75th	**5** 76th
6 77th	**1** 78th	**6** 79th	**5** 80th	**4** 81st	**8** 82nd	**2** 83rd
6 84th	**3** 85th	**3** 86th	**7** 87th	**6** 88th	**7** 89th	**22** 90th

MIXED MESSAGES

Tattooists have done rather well out of football. Rare is the player who doesn't treat his body as a canvas for a tribute to mum, kids, wife, girlfriend or other source of inspiration. Inked-on pieces of symbolism also abound – but what does it all mean?

TIM HOWARD
COLORADO RAPIDS & USA
The goalkeeper is covered in tattoos, including dragons, a crucifix, a Superman logo, his grandfather in military uniform and a young version of his mother.

DANIELE DE ROSSI
AS ROMA & ITALY
A triangular 'warning' sign on the back of De Rossi's leg plays up to his aggressive reputation. It shows a standing figure stepping on the leg of another, prostrate, figure.

RAUL MEIRELES
PORTUGAL
The midfielder's footballing career unfolds on his right leg in a collection of pictures. It includes the Torre dos Clérigos in his home town Porto, a Portuguese cable car and fado guitar, the Blue Mosque in Istanbul and a British red telephone box.

THIERRY HENRY
The former Arsenal, Barcelona, New York Red Bulls and France player is a devotee of the tattoo. The length of his left arm is a tribute first to his daughter, Téa, and then to New York, with depictions of the Empire State Building and Brooklyn Bridge.

RAHEEM STERLING
MANCHESTER CITY & ENGLAND

On Sterling's arm, an image of a 10-year-old boy stares up at the famous arch of Wembley Stadium, with the words 'It's a dream'. Sterling lived close to the stadium when he was a boy.

LIONEL MESSI
BARCELONA & ARGENTINA

Messi has the name of his son, Thiago, etched on the back of his left calf, below two hands.

DAVID BECKHAM
ENGLAND

Becks now has more than 40 tattoos, including multiple cherubs and the name of his wife, Victoria, in Sanskrit.

NIGEL DE JONG
GALATASARAY & NETHERLANDS

The Indonesian body artist Ade Itameda designed De Jong's traditional warrior tattoos.

SERGIO RAMOS
REAL MADRID & SPAIN

On the back of Ramos's left calf is the Champions League trophy, while on the back of his right calf is the World Cup trophy.

SERGIO AGÜERO
MANCHESTER CITY & ARGENTINA

The inside of Agüero's right forearm bears his name – in Elvish.

NO, THANK YOU!
CRISTIANO RONALDO
REAL MADRID & PORTUGAL

Completely tattoo-less – like all blood donors, Ronaldo is advised not to indulge in body art or piercings for at least some time afterwards to avoid potential infection.

WHO PLAYS IN WHAT?

Football is a colourful game and that extends to what the players of different countries wear, which in turn is reflected in the displays put on by fans. On the next four pages is a quick visual guide to the team colours for all exisiting nations that have appeared in World Cups.

NORTH AMERICA ———— | ———— EUROPE

CANADA	COSTA RICA	REPUBLIC OF IRELAND	PORTUGAL
USA	CUBA	NORTHERN IRELAND	SPAIN
MEXICO	HAITI	SCOTLAND	FRANCE
EL SALVADOR	JAMAICA	ENGLAND	NETHERLANDS
HONDURAS	TRINIDAD & TOBAGO	WALES	BELGIUM

continued overleaf

GERMANY

CZECH REPUBLIC

BULGARIA

SERBIA

DENMARK

SLOVAKIA

ROMANIA

UKRAINE

NORWAY

SWITZERLAND

CROATIA

RUSSIA

SWEDEN

AUSTRIA

SLOVENIA

ITALY

POLAND

HUNGARY

BOSNIA & HERZEGOVINA

GREECE

EUROPE | SOUTH AMERICA | AFRICA

TURKEY

ISRAEL

ECUADOR

PERU

CHILE

COLOMBIA

BOLIVIA

BRAZIL

ARGENTINA

PARAGUAY

URUGUAY

SENEGAL

IVORY COAST

GHANA

TOGO

NIGERIA

ANGOLA

CAMEROON

EGYPT

SAUDI ARABIA

NORTH KOREA

DR CONGO

KUWAIT

SOUTH KOREA

SOUTH AFRICA

UNITED ARAB EMIRATES

JAPAN

MOROCCO

IRAQ

INDONESIA

ALGERIA

IRAN

AUSTRALIA

TUNISIA

CHINA PR

NEW ZEA!

Brimming with creative inspiration, how-to projects and useful information to enrich your everyday life, Quarto Knows is a favourite destination for those pursuing their interests and passions. Visit our site and dig deeper with our books into your area of interest: Quarto Creates, Quarto Cooks, Quarto Homes, Quarto Lives, Quarto Drives, Quarto Explores, Quarto Gifts, or Quarto Kids.

ACKNOWLEDGEMENTS

Useful websites

The following websites are good sources of information for all things football-related.

Governing bodies:

fifa.com; uefa.com; cafonline.com; conmebol.com; concacaf.com; the-afc.com

Leagues:

premierleague.com; bundesliga.com; laliga.es; ligue1.com; cbf.com.br; mlssoccer.com; jleague.jp; kleague.com; a-league.com.au

Media:

bbc.co.uk/sport/0/football; espnfc.com; fourfourtwo.com; francefootball.fr; skysports.com/football; talksport.com; worldsoccer.com

Online stats and facts:

11v11.com; 90min.com; bleacherreport.com/world-football; caughtoffside.com; footballdatabase.eu; forbes.com/sports-leisure; goal.com; guinnessworldrecords.com; livestrong. com/sscat/soccer; planetworldcup.com; shortlist.com/ entertainment/sport; soccerlens.com; stadiumguide.com; statbunker.com; therichest.com/category/sports/soccer-sports; totalsportek.com/category/football; tsmplug.com/category/ football; whoateallthepies.tv; whoscored.com

Image credits:

Tim Brown: 12, 13, 160, 161
Bill Donohoe: 12, 13, 60, 61, 64, 65, 70, 71, 80, 92, 93, 104,
6, 127, 136, 137, 151
iel Nyari: 1, 2, 16, 31, 37, 40, 54, 56, 59, 68, 69, 79, 84,
3, 107, 109, 124, 129, 140, 145, 154, 163, 167, 173,
186
12, 36, 54, 55, 56, 57, 94, 128, 129
oted from artworks © Shutterstock.com

First published in 2016 by Aurum Press
an imprint of The Quarto Group
The Old Brewery
6 Blundell Street
London N7 9BH
United Kingdom

www.QuartoKnows.com

This revised and updated paperback edition first published in 2017 by Aurum Press

Every effort has been made to verify the accuracy of data up to the end of the 2015–16 football seasons. Some statistics will inevitably change over time, but the publishers will be glad to rectify in future edtions any omissions brought in writing to their attention. Some statistics will change quicker than others. please refer to the credited sources for latest information.

A catalogue record for this book is available from the British Library.

UK Edition ISBN 978 1 78131 668 9
North American Edition ISBN 978 1 78131 667 2

10 9 8 7 6 5 4 3 2
2021 2020 2019 2018 2017

Text by John Andrews
Design: www.fogdog.co.uk
Player portraits: Daniel Nyari
Infographic illustration: Tim Brown, Nick Clark, Bill Donohoe, Jane McKenna, Paul Oakley

Printed in China

CAMEROON

EGYPT

SAUDI ARABIA

NORTH KOREA

DR CONGO

KUWAIT

SOUTH KOREA

SOUTH AFRICA

UNITED ARAB EMIRATES

JAPAN

MOROCCO

IRAQ

INDONESIA

ALGERIA

IRAN

AUSTRALIA

TUNISIA

CHINA PR

NEW ZEALAND

Brimming with creative inspiration, how-to projects and useful information to enrich your everyday life, Quarto Knows is a favourite destination for those pursuing their interests and passions. Visit our site and dig deeper with our books into your area of interest: Quarto Creates, Quarto Cooks, Quarto Homes, Quarto Lives, Quarto Drives, Quarto Explores, Quarto Gifts, or Quarto Kids.

ACKNOWLEDGEMENTS

Useful websites

The following websites are good sources of information for all things football-related.

Governing bodies:

fifa.com; uefa.com; cafonline.com; conmebol.com; concacaf.com; the-afc.com

Leagues:

premierleague.com; bundesliga.com; laliga.es; ligue1.com; cbf.com.br; mlssoccer.com; jleague.jp; kleague.com; a-league.com.au

Media:

bbc.co.uk/sport/0/football; espnfc.com; fourfourtwo.com; francefootball.fr; skysports.com/football; talksport.com; worldsoccer.com

Online stats and facts:

11v11.com; 90min.com; bleacherreport.com/world-football; caughtoffside.com; footballdatabase.eu; forbes.com/sports-leisure; goal.com; guinnessworldrecords.com; livestrong.com/sscat/soccer; planetworldcup.com; shortlist.com/entertainment/sport; soccerlens.com; stadiumguide.com; statbunker.com; therichest.com/category/sports/soccer-sports; totalsportek.com/category/football; tsmplug.com/category/football; whoateallthepies.tv; whoscored.com

Image credits:

Tim Brown: 12, 13, 160, 161
Bill Donohoe: 12, 13, 60, 61, 64, 65, 70, 71, 80, 92, 93, 104, 126, 127, 136, 137, 151
© Daniel Nyari: 1, 2, 16, 31, 37, 40, 54, 56, 59, 68, 69, 79, 84, 85, 90, 103, 107, 109, 124, 129, 140, 145, 154, 163, 167, 173, 174, 180, 185, 186
Paul Oakley: 11, 12, 36, 54, 55, 56, 57, 94, 128, 129
All other images adapted from artworks © Shutterstock.com

First published in 2016 by Aurum Press
an imprint of The Quarto Group
The Old Brewery
6 Blundell Street
London N7 9BH
United Kingdom

www.QuartoKnows.com

This revised and updated paperback edition first published in 2017 by Aurum Press

Copyright © 2016, 2017 Quarto Publishing plc.
Text © 2016, 2017 Aurum Press

Every effort has been made to verify the accuracy of data up to the end of the 2015–16 football seasons. Some statistics will inevitably change over time, but the publishers will be glad to rectify in future edtions any omissions brought in writing to their attention. Some statistics will change quicker than others. please refer to the credited sources for latest information.

A catalogue record for this book is available from the British Library.

UK Edition ISBN 978 1 78131 668 9
North American Edition ISBN 978 1 78131 667 2

10 9 8 7 6 5 4 3 2
2021 2020 2019 2018 2017

Text by John Andrews
Design: www.fogdog.co.uk
Player portraits: Daniel Nyari
Infographic illustration: Tim Brown, Nick Clark, Bill Donohoe, Jane McKenna, Paul Oakley

Printed in China